Living Fully

LIVING FULLY:

A Guide for Young People with
a Handicap, Their Parents,
Their Teachers, and Professionals

Sol Gordon

The John Day Company

Designed by Ingrid Beckman

Manufactured in the United States of America

Library of Congress Cataloging in Publication Data

Main entry under title:

Living fully.

    Includes index.
    1. Handicapped children—Addresses, essays, lectures. 2. Handicapped children—Family relationships—Addresses, essays, lectures. I. Gordon, Sol, 1923–
HV888.L58 1975   362.7′8′4   75-25984
ISBN 0-381-98283-1

10 9 8 7 6 5 4 3 2 1

Sarah Jane Atwood is a self-employed person with a handicap, and is currently working on a book about her experiences.

Douglas P. Biklen is an Assistant Professor in Special Education and coordinator of advocacy at the Center on Human Policy at Syracuse University.

Ronald S. Horowitz is a high school teacher in Princeton, New Jersey, who is involved in developing alternative opportunities within public schools.

Betty Lou Kratoville is a well-known writer in the field of learning disabilities and is director of the Archway School in Houston, Texas.

James P. Lynch is an activist member of Disabled in Action, a teacher, and speaker on rights issues for people who are physically disabled.

Philip Schnipper is a student at SUNY in Albany preparing for a career in speech and hearing.

Charles Weening was formerly associated with a state rehabilitation commission and is coordinator of a child-study team in Jersey City, New Jersey.

Ruth Wessler is a psychotherapist and the editor of *Rational Living*, a publication of the Institute for Rational Living.

Acknowledgment

I wish to acknowledge the valuable assistance of Craig W. Snyder, who helped me get this book together. Thanks are also due to the contributors whose experiences enhance this book.

Contents

II For Parents and Families

III For Professionals

IV For All of Us

V Resources

Foreword

What does one hope for in a writer? What does the true writer hope for in himself? It's O.K. not to write, not to commit one's thinking to public exposure and judgment. But, if one does write, writing must be judged on its style and substance—not either, both. Although there isn't one without the other—where style molds the substance and, out of the matter of writing, form is created—something must hold it all together. That something is sincerity encased in honesty, and that's Sol Gordon's long suit. But, his writing has another powerful virtue. To write with passion is to risk everything and, frankly, gain little. Yet, for some, to write at all is to write with passion. Professor Gordon is not afraid to write with passion; in fact, I truly believe it's his preferred rhythm and color of expression. However, lest the reader conclude from all of this—especially in light of the subject of this book, handicapped people, and what the editor is

most known for, sex education—that here is a book whose
words are sad and pessimistic or never rise above the crotch, let
me hasten to add that, whenever Sol Gordon writes or
coordinates the efforts of colleagues, good things happen in the
readers' heads and hearts and souls.

First the subject, now the object, for it is reasonable for you
to expect me to say something about this particular book, *Living
Fully.* I hesitate a bit because there are some books that speak
better for themselves than through interpreters. I think that this
is that kind of book. Nevertheless, I will say something now, but
I'll try not to spoil it for you. This is a "different" book by and
about people who, unfortunately, are thought of as being
different. It's full of surprises, maybe shocks—as well as
inspiration, guidance, and information. It's without the types of
prejudices that are even more debilitating than the so-called
handicaps it seeks to help us better comprehend; and that's a
real surprise in this age of labeling, cynical pessimism, and the
rampant segregation of unwanted people. It presents many
perspectives, those of the "victims" themselves as well as those
of our professional colleagues. It offers both "how to do it"
approaches as well as "why it needs to be done" rationales. It
has substance and depth and thoughtfulness—terms that are
usually just clichés but, here, denote honest and wonderful
accomplishments. It provides people—all people, especially
young men and women who feel different—with a beginning for
changing themselves, for believing that each of us is a valuable
person, and that the earth is ours for us to shape for human
beings and for human needs. It exemplifies its own first lesson:
Don't settle; get it all together; everything is here for people to
make of their lives what they want and what they will work for.
So read this book and, probably, you will learn, as I have
learned—not exactly as I have learned but as fulfillingly. And,
the message is clear: All lives are fragile, and life itself is never
without risks and disappointments. Yet, whatever the circum-

stances, one improves his prospects as an independent citizen. Therefore, each person must be guaranteed opportunities to be truly free. Read this book, and you may more than survive, and even be more than free. Read it, and you may learn how to help others and contribute to their lives. That is the ultimate experience.

For some people, being honest is very hard work indeed; for Sol Gordon, it's both his strength and his way of life. And, while I had to mention something about this book, I also have to conclude this preface by saying that honesty itself isn't always sufficient to be appreciated; sometimes, it's painful to others, or annoying, or draining, or sanctimonious. With Sol Gordon, honesty is usually welcomed and, often, delightful. Why? While, for some, their central objective—their "thing"—is power and honors, for Sol it has always been just friendship and people and doing good things for them.

January 1975
Jamesville, New York

Burton Blatt
Centennial Professor and Director
Division of Special Education and Rehabilitation
Syracuse University

Our Philosophy

In an increasingly complex world, the problems of youth who have handicaps have become more compelling. Often isolated, neglected, undereducated, and most devastating, un- or inappropriately employed, the person finds his or her handicap emerging as the minor burden compared to feelings of worthlessness and despair.

Our book is designed mainly to enhance the self-acceptance of youths with handicaps who are of at least potentially average intelligence and who are, for the most part, capable of taking care of themselves. We include the majority of the cerebral-palsied, blind, deaf, epileptic, learning-disabled, neurogically and otherwise physically handicapped persons, as well as the chronically ill and emotionally disturbed. (Parents of retarded youth can also profit from this book, although their problems will not be our principal concern.) The main focus will be on those who can read or comprehend sections of this book by themselves and who could be expected to marry (if they wanted to), adequately function in families or in group homes, and be productively employed.

In this sense, whether it's called normalization or mainstreaming, integrating the person with a handicap into all aspects of society remains the overriding goal. We write with the full recognition that mainstreaming often requires training, preparation, readiness, and transitional phases from segregation to integration. This is not to say that no facility should remain homogeneous, but rather when possible, people who have handicaps should be tried in the mainstream. The responsibility lies with the schools and rehabilitation services and public facilities in all communities.

Perhaps, for a small number of people, segregated activities would be an appropriate lifestyle, though it's hard for us to imagine any person who could not fit into the mainstream in some aspect of his or her life. It is not an all-or-nothing process. But the feeling of being part of things is essential to mental health and self-acceptance.

While each of the chapters is written for a specific group, youth and young adults, their parents, teachers, and related professionals would profit from reading the entire book and talking things over with each other. In this sense our book is unique and avoids the usual pitfalls of writing about instead of to the person concerned. The book addresses people who have handicaps, not people who are handicapped. We have not used (we trust) the usual professional jargon and technical terms.

Our book is dedicated to the idea that how people with handicaps feel about themselves will be the most important factor in their adult adjustment or maladjustment—recognizing that one of the most important contributing factors will be how society treats its most vulnerable citizens.

We will focus on everyday problems of school and home

"management," concentrating on basic socialization needs which will enhance opportunities for adult happiness.

For some parents the main problem is irrational guilt, and for many more a society that often does not care about its citizens who have handicaps.

For many people with handicaps the biggest problem is self-pity and boredom.

For many professionals our least forgivable shortcoming is the tendency to be patronizing and making the assumption that parents don't know as much as we do, or sometimes forgetting that we are part of the society that neglects people with handicaps.

Thus, it is in the spirit of "Let's get it together" that this book is written.

There are no substitutes for friends, things one can do well, a choice of activities in one's leisure, and knowledge of oneself and of life in the broadest sense.

We salute people with handicaps who are "making it" or have gotten it together. This book is really for those who have not—and want to very much.

Living Fully

I

For the People
Who Have Handicaps

1

Even Though It's Hard Having a Handicap— Select, Don't Settle!

As a person with a handicap, your worst problem is probably thinking you aren't as good as everybody else. If someone sees, talks, walks, or hears better than you do, you might find yourself thinking "I'm stupid . . . worthless. Why did this happen to me?"

Unless it happened in an accident after you were born, usually nobody knows why it happened to you. Besides, does it matter whose "fault" it was? Knowing that won't solve any problems. It's tough to have a handicap. Some things are harder for you to do than for other people, and there are some things you can't do at all. This does not mean that you can't do *anything* well.

I'm going to be as straightforward as I can in this chapter. I'll be saying some things most people would be afraid to tell you. You might become angry with me, but that doesn't matter as long as you think seriously about what I say. Some of what I write won't apply to your own situation and experience, but give the rest of it a chance. Even if it hurts to admit some things, you may be able to use this knowledge to help yourself. The Council for Exceptional Children (CEC) estimates that there are about six million school-age students with handicaps serious enough to warrant special attention. Though it doesn't really improve your situation, it can be a comfort to know that you aren't alone.

Some people may tell you things like "We're all handicapped in some way." This may be technically true, but it doesn't help matters any. If you have no friends, you might hear "everybody likes you," but you probably know that this isn't true either.

The truth is, few people are going to like you unless you like yourself. Just having a handicap isn't enough to inspire friendships, and few people want to be with you if you feel sorry for yourself and complain a lot. In many ways, the advice I offer refers to anybody. Nothing is more of a burden than to let people know how inferior you feel or how tough life is on you—these feelings can become more of a burden for you than the handicap itself. The highest level of unhappiness is apparent when a person declares, "I have nothing to do, nobody likes me, I have nothing to say."

I hope you won't think it sounds corny when I tell you that there are plenty of things you can do. But you have to be imaginative! If you can't play baseball or participate in athletics, don't waste time being sad. Instead, look for things you *can* do. You'll only hurt yourself if you pretend that you can do everything.

The first steps are to develop interests and hobbies to give you something fun to do and talk about. It doesn't matter if it is music, art, photography, stamps, coins, cooking, sewing, games, reading, or whatever. Having several strong interests of your own makes you interesting to other people with similar interests because they can exchange ideas with you. If you are a chess player others will want to play you. If you play an instrument maybe you could get together with other musicians and jam. What counts is an active interest—just liking television isn't particularly interesting to others, although it can be a topic of conversation. The best way to learn about people and activities is to talk with people. Share past experiences, ideas and philosophies, interests. Conversation is a learned art. If you don't know what to say, listen to what other people are saying.

How do you feel about reading? One of the worst things that can happen to anyone is not to enjoy reading. I understand that your parents, teachers, and counselors may have forced you to read and consequently you may have developed a dislike for it; yet, there are few better ways to spend time alone than reading. At the end of this book I have a reading list with selections that I think almost any teenager or young adult would enjoy.

Despite everything you've tried in the past, choose two or three of these books to read when you want to and see if reading by yourself without teachers, pressure, and grades isn't really fun. If books are too long, try comics, short stories, plays, newspapers. There are magazines for almost every person imaginable.

Don't get upset because you think I'm asking you to do a lot of unreasonable things. When I was teaching in high school, I assigned new experiences. Here is a typical assignment from those days:

You are required, in order to pass this course, to have several new experiences. Write a brief psychological report on three such experiences you have actually had. Choose from the following:

   1. Even if you don't like poetry (or perhaps *particularly* if you don't like poetry), read a poem carefully from beginning to end. What is the poet saying to you?

2. If you think of yourself as a liberal in political and social terms, read from cover to cover an issue of *The National Review*.

3. If you are conservatively inclined, read from cover to cover an issue of *The New Republic*, *The Nation*, or *The Humanist*.

4. If the only time you've ever been to an art museum is when someone (a parent? a teacher?) dragged you into one, visit a large art museum. Spend part of your time trying to figure out why people voluntarily visit art museums.

5. Attend a ballet performance.

6. Sit through an entire opera, such as *Aida*. Or, if this is not possible, listen to a recording of an entire opera.

7. Obtain a copy of the Sunday *New York Times*, and spend four hours finding out why it is one of the world's most prestigious newspapers.

8. If your everyday personality inclines to be grumpy, spend a whole day deliberately being nice to people.

9. If you have not been getting along well with your parents recently, try being really polite to them for two days. (Politeness is sort of a formula for achieving a little harmonious distance in personal relations. It isn't an end in itself but rather a preliminary to getting closer together— or moving farther apart.)

10. If you have the conviction that people should love you for what you are, rather than for how you dress or act, try dressing and acting conventionally for a week. Note carefully the responses you get from people who you assumed were either indifferent or hostile.

What is the point of all this? Simply that whatever you may decide to do with your life, the choice should be made on the basis of a wide range of possible alternatives. If your experience is constricting or routinized, you may miss out on some of the very best possibilities open to you. Above all, don't decide in advance on the things you hate and will always hate.

In short, get out of your rut (if you are in one).

Here are some other things you can try:

Keep a diary.
Remember dreams.
Learn a new word each day.
Photograph trees.
Photograph people.
Write one poem.
Write two poems.
Fly a kite.
Say hello to a person you think you should hate.
Write a letter to your Congressman on something you really care about.
Choose a foreign country to visit. Learn as much as you can about it. (Later on you can worry about how you're going to get there.)
Write me a letter.
See a foreign film.

Here is a list of things I like:

My wife because I can count on her.
Traveling to places I've never been to before.
Cracking jokes.
Eating out in elegant restaurants, especially when I can't afford it.
The songs of my religion.
Reading a "heavy" novel very slowly.
Sending out vibrations to people who strike my fancy.
Going to the movies and seeing a film like *Harold and Maude*.
Talking intimately with close friends.
Listening to old-time jazz records by myself.

Bittersweet chocolates.

Coin collecting.

Daydreaming.

Making up slogans like "Cheap is expensive" and "If God is dead, She must have been alive once."

If you don't have any ideas of your own, ask other people what they enjoy doing. Finding one thing to start with is usually the hardest step.

Become an "expert" in something. If you like music, study and listen to it, read about the composers, or play an instrument. Like reading? Find an author you think really knows something and read all his or her books. People like to talk with other people who know what they're talking about.

Some of you may have already tried a few of the things I've suggested and the experiment failed. Your first attempts might have been when you weren't even ready for them. Now you may find it easier to do difficult or new things by yourself or with just one other person in a relaxed setting. Then you won't have to worry about people watching or feeling that you have to please somebody else.

Perhaps you are afraid to join groups or clubs because you anticipate being unwanted, laughed at, or discriminated against. More often than not organizations will welcome your membership, but sometimes it's a struggle—you have to make people give you what is your right. In a way it's like the struggle of minority groups in our country to be recognized: Blacks, Jews, Puerto Ricans, and others. Strangers are suspect, as are people who look, act, or talk differently. Each of us can help by accepting each other the way we are.

One other thing you must do is keep yourself in shape and looking attractive. It is just as important for a blind person or someone in a wheelchair to keep fit as it is for a long-distance runner. If you let your body go downhill, you may feel ugly and undesirable. Anything from isometrics to swimming does the job, and choosing what you enjoy best is half the fun. Be imaginative—if you're in a wheelchair you may be able to play Ping-Pong, billiards, and possibly even learn to swim or lift weights. Don't decide that you really can't do something unless you've tried hard.

Just as important as being healthy is looking your best. If you don't keep yourself looking nice, you'll probably wind up thinking less of yourself. You'd be surprised at what a lift it is to make an effort to present yourself well to others. People confined to a bed or wheelchair tend to gain weight from overeating. Excessive intake of food is one of the worst ways to deal with problems, for in the end you only suffer more from being overweight. Using food, tobacco, alcohol, TV, or drugs to reduce anxieties which are symptoms of problems not being dealt with in a constructive way is self-destructive. Instead of helping themselves face reality, people hurt their bodies and/or minds with these things. Besides, a drinking problem or overeating is like double punishment—why compound one problem with others? Still, one always tells another person to give up habits with tongue in cheek. We're not against food, tobacco, alcohol, TV, or drugs per se, but being "controlled" by them is what's bad.

You've probably lived with your handicap long enough by now to get a real sense of the easiest way to get things done. For example, a desk with a rim around the edge that keeps things from falling off may keep you from bending over a lot. Arranging the furniture in your room a certain way, railings where you might need them, and other devices and methods are all ways you might be able to do things with less effort. If you can't write, a tape recorder would fill the same purpose. If you discover helpful ideas, talk them over with your parents and teachers and see if they can be implemented. Even if it's something very simple, don't be afraid to mention it because it might give you more time to enjoy other things.

Some people with handicaps don't like the idea of using any aids or devices that would make things easier for them, even in their own homes. They feel that since none of these things exists in public or anywhere outside their homes, they should get used to being without them. "There are no railings in public schools, so why have them at home?" I've been asked. This is more or less up to the individual, but I tend to feel that one's home is for comfort and unless you don't, for instance, already know how to get around without railings, there's no harm in them.

Some of you, I'm sure, have developed an instinctive resistance to comments, suggestions, or criticism made by adults. Maybe this is because you thought they were ordering you around, or you suspected they had their own better interests in mind instead of yours. You may feel this way about parents, teachers, relatives, counselors, or just about any older person. If you're used to "turning off" their advice, what do you suppose might happen if you followed it for a while, say a week? It wouldn't mean giving up your personality or integrity—you'd just be listening to others, experimenting. It's hard to admit, but sometimes other people know better than ourselves what's right for us, just as we sometimes know better than they do what's right for them.

And, of course, some of you have good relationships with your parents. But many of you, in addition to almost everybody else, don't get along with your parents at different stages of your lives. Since people with handicaps are usually more dependent on their parents and spend more time at home than the average person, it's especially important for them to get along with their parents. I certainly appreciate the possibility that parents mean well but don't always do or say the right thing. Sometimes they are too involved in structuring your life for you. But obviously, if you can organize your own life's activities and interests, you'll find there is less criticism and difficulty getting things done.

Part of getting along with your parents involves being polite. In fact, if you are really polite, it will develop some distance between you instead of making you more dependent. If you don't believe it, try it and you'll see what I mean. At a later stage, you may want to be considerate and understanding. This takes a lot more effort than politeness and will probably get you more respect in return.

Another aspect of family life is brothers and sisters. If you have any, you know how much fun they can be, and also what a hassle at times. It is really important for everybody in the family to understand each other's feelings. They might feel you receive more attention from your parents than they do, and they want an equal share too. Make a special effort to ask them if they feel deprived because of your problem. Then, without asking for special consideration or pity, figure out a way you can get along. Again, if you try to understand their point of view, hopefully they'll try to understand yours.

You might feel at some time that because of your handicap you are a burden to your family. You might feel guilty or ashamed to feel this way too. But you know, every thought you could possibly have is all right. Most people think about suicide at some point in their lives when nothing is going right. All thoughts are normal! Behavior can be wrong, but not thoughts. If your impulses and thoughts are mainly voluntary and enjoyable, and you don't frequently daydream instead of doing real things, there's no problem. Even if you sometimes wish somebody harm, have strange sexual thoughts about rape, sadism, or whatever, there is no reason to worry. Just remember that if you feel guilty about a thought, you will have the thought over and over again. If the thought of having sex with your brother or sister once bothered you, did you notice that you kept having the same thought? If you can just accept the troublesome thought, though, it will soon go away. Guilt is the reason why thoughts become involuntary—obsessive is the way psychologists describe it.

It goes without saying that most people wish you weren't handicapped. This is because they care and know things would be easier for you. If your parents, brothers and sisters, and friends didn't care, it wouldn't matter to them how you did things. You can say, "Nobody cares about me," but inside you know you don't mean it. Sure, some people probably don't care and will be mean, but that's their problem, not yours. Remember, too, no one can make you feel inferior without your consent.

2

The Psychology of Having a Handicap

This may sound like a strange title, but I use it because there are certain things you must know that nonhandicapped people don't have to worry about. It is very important for you to realize that people who have been made fun of, ridiculed, discriminated against, and heavily criticized sometimes react by being negative and unpleasant to others. Sometimes we express our hostility only to the people who care about us the most. It is really hard to be nice if others reject you and won't let you in their groups. If you tend to be hostile, even the people who are your friends or who would like to be your friends will feel rejected by you though you don't really want them to feel that way. A sure sign we are doing something wrong is if we become meaner and meaner to the people we are closest to or who care about us the most. That's why, despite your own unhappiness and experiences, showing compassion and understanding to others, especially other people who have handicaps, is so important. At times you'll have to struggle with your anger and sometimes you'll show how mad you are anyway. If you're religious, it can help to remember that behaving in a loving way toward others is in God's spirit.

People tend to call one another unfriendly names. They have done this for hundreds and thousands of years all over the world. When angry, upset, or just feeling mean, people tend to lash out with words like "stupid." Such name calling is always hurtful, and in the case of persons with handicaps, it can be worse because they already have doubts about their own mental or physical abilities. But just because someone blurts it out doesn't make it true. The important thing is not to believe any foolish statements or labels that are hurled in the middle of an angry quarrel, or by an unfriendly stranger you don't even know.

Any way you look at it, having a sense of humor is looser and more fun than being uptight. Clichés like "Have a nice day" and "Inside every cloud there's a silver lining" may sound phony, but there's a point to them: Troubled people often lose their sense of humor. They get so wound up in their problems and the bad side of life that they rarely reach up and out of their holes to see what the rest of the world is doing.

We've probably all been in the situation of trying to brighten someone's gloom. The conversation may go something like this:

"Hey, what's the matter?"

"Everything, man. I don't know what to do."

"Do you want to talk about it?"

"No."

"Do you feel like doing anything? It might help to get out."

"Not really. I just want to be alone."

Of course, sometimes the person says, "Great, I need a change of pace."

Moody people are usually depressed and don't let themselves

feel good often enough. Forcing a smile or faking being in a good mood may not seem natural at first, but sometimes we must mechanically learn things before they become spontaneous. Sometimes we react with "How do they do it?" when we see happy people, and it's probably due to a positive outlook more than anything else. The key is understanding that it is possible to maintain humor even when situations in our lives don't turn out as well as we had hoped. When you get down to it, there's probably some humor and sadness in every situation.

Another psychological principle relates to new relationships. Since it may be more difficult for you to get out and make new friends, when the opportunity presents itself you may tend to rush things and try to get as close as possible to the other person in as short a time as possible. The people may be adults, teachers, or fellow students who want to befriend you too. As a rule, proceed slowly even though you may be anxious to get together quickly. Even if they are pleasant and want to be friends, don't assume they'll be around all the time or that you'll be best friends immediately. Saying things like "I had a really good time today . . . see you again soon" are conventional but keep the relationship alive without coming on too strong. If you give the impression that you absolutely must have the person as a friend, well, most people find that to be a burden.

It is rarely a good idea to demand love, care, and attention from your family, friends, or anyone else—you have to earn it by offering love first. This includes doing your share of work if possible (Don't *ever* try to get out of doing something you can do by thinking "I can't because I'm handicapped"), being considerate of others' feelings and efforts, showing appreciation, as well as doing your best to learn and mature.

A good deal of the love people receive when they are young comes from their parents. They love to hug and kiss their kids, embrace, and show affection with their children. Sometimes relatives and very close friends do these things too, and most people enjoy the good feelings very much. But sometimes these people feel so sorry for people with handicaps that they want to give more love and affection than most people usually share. Thus, the handicapped person may grow up believing that most people do these things, maybe even casual acquaintances or strangers. They may be hurt or confused when people reject their physical affection. It is important for all people to realize that hugs and kisses usually belong only between people who are relatives or close friends. Of course, people with visual disabilities rely more on the sense of touch in getting to know people, and should only be sure that other people understand this.

As an adolescent or young adult, chances are you are looking forward to an intimate relationship with someone of the opposite sex. This is perfectly natural and something that you'll enjoy and cherish. But from my experience, people who have trouble relating to members of their own sex don't succeed any better with the opposite sex. In effect, you'll be happiest if you develop the ability to understand members of your own sex first (it's usually easier) and use this as the foundation for expanding your relationships and experiences to the other sex as well.

To make friends with anybody, though, you have to begin with liking yourself. What you think of yourself depends a lot on how you spend your time and your relationships with other people. If you see yourself as little more than a charity case, a burden, or an inconvenience, chances are you don't think you're worth much at all. This kind of thinking can make you afraid to mature and to make your own decisions and do things for yourself. People often ask, "But how do I start liking myself?" Sometimes, it's easiest to begin by liking one thing in particular: the way you feel about other people, the way you paint, sing, debate, your looks, or whatever. Once you've found just one thing, you'll discover many more. It will feel much better to know you *can* do something worthwhile instead of worrying that you *can't* do something else.

You may find that the best way to begin making friends in the community at large is to start with other people who have handicaps. Despite your own possible reluctance, I would say this is a good start. Most communities have programs, workshops, or projects for helping people with handicaps, and there's no reason to feel bad about participating—you aren't causing trouble or wasting anyone's time. It's possible that once you become familiar with these organizations and their procedures you'll want to volunteer some of your time to help other people besides yourself. At least give it a try, and you'll discover the same good feeling it gives other people to lend you a hand.

Sometimes people might talk or act toward you differently because of your handicap. A friend of mine tells the story of taking a friend who is blind to get registered for a college course. When they got to the registration desk, the woman there addressed all her questions about the registration to the sighted person instead of his blind companion. She said, for instance, "Is he a freshman, sophomore, junior, or senior?" And, "Is he going to pay now or later? Where is his transcript?" The blind person was perfectly capable of answering all her questions for himself but the woman acted as if for some reason he couldn't! He should have said, "Excuse me, but would you please ask me instead?"

It is important to let people know how capable you are. You can't expect every stranger on the street to understand what you can and can't do. Even people who know you probably underestimate your abilities at times, so you have to tell them and demonstrate in actions what you can do. Don't just get depressed or angry when people shortchange you or even when they make nasty or inconsiderate remarks. It's certainly not your fault that some people won't make allowances, don't try to understand, and make harsh judgments. It is appropriate to respond to some of these people, but the obviously mean ones or one-time encounters are best ignored.

For most handicapped teenagers and young adults, school is a real problem. Whether it's in the form of regular classroom instruction, part-time schooling, special classes, programs and projects, school away from home, or private tutoring in the home, school is often disliked for numerous reasons. You may be asked to do things you don't enjoy or actually can't do. Maybe the time periods are too short or too long and you aren't allowed to do what really interests you the most. Possibly your teacher doesn't understand your needs and misinterprets why you do things the way you do.

It is easier and more fun to do things we like than those we don't enjoy as much. Maybe for you chess is more fun than doing dishes, gardening more fun than TV, history better than French, or whatever. We all have our preferences. But if you dislike school most of the time, you know how tiring it is to be there. You may not like school better by trying to work harder and understand things, but in any case, there are some ways to get along better in the school system.

If some aspect of school or subjects displeases you or is difficult for you to perform, explain why and suggest alternate methods. Remember, people are more willing to listen to complaints if they are explained and talked over instead of your just getting angry and upset. If you can keep in mind how important it is to learn some things—not necessarily everything that is taught—you'll be better able to accept what is presented in class. Even if you must go more slowly than other students, learning is what counts. At least try to see the goal of a diploma or an education if you can't enjoy school's daily routine. Unfortunately, many young people don't discover how hard it is for a dropout to find a job until after they've dropped out.

This is more of a problem for people with handicaps than for nonhandicapped. Whereas 14 percent of the total U.S. population failed to complete eighth grade, the figure is 22 percent for the handicapped. And only 5 percent of people with handicaps finished four or more years of college compared with 9 percent for the total population.

In addition, 21 percent of handicapped persons are living below the poverty level, compared to a general 14 percent for others. About 42 percent of the adults who have handicaps are employed while 53 percent of the rest of the population is (President's Commission on Employment of the Handicapped).

Furthermore, the U.S. Census Bureau reports (1972) that income reflected the level of education:

Less than 8 years	$280,000
Grade school completed	$345,000
High school—1 to 3 years	$390,000
High school completed	$480,000
College—1 to 3 years	$545,000
College completed	$710,000
College—5 years or more	$825,000

These figures are estimated total income from age eighteen to death for males; the estimates for females would be considerably less.

The importance of education cannot be overstated in terms of income, self-confidence, and responsiveness of employers. In light of the fact that people with handicaps must struggle harder for education and employment, the decision to remain in school is a wise one for most, but of course not all, people.

We've already discussed the things you may not like about school, so now let's explore possible things you do like (whether you like to admit it or not). Maybe you like the teacher(s), some of the other students, a few of the subjects (nobody likes them all), the people who work in the cafeteria, the janitor, the principal, and hopefully learning in itself.

I think you'll find that being realistic about your abilities and limitations will cause people to cooperate. For instance, if you'd like to get into a game of baseball and you've hardly ever played, a good way to get involved might be to say, "Listen, I know I'm not very good, but I'd like to try and learn"—and you'll almost always be let in the game. A little humor and joking around can usually loosen everyone up too.

As you get older and start thinking about graduating from high school or college, you'll probably wonder about jobs. Let's face it, there is a lot of discrimination against handicapped people in the job market. Some employers are afraid to take a "chance" with a person with a handicap or are afraid that the "image" of their company will suffer. They just don't know any better, but that doesn't help you get a job. Some people with handicaps are very successful at their work, and it usually takes some imagination (for anyone) to get a fulfilling job.

There are two points I want to emphasize. One is, if you are bored most of the time, you are boring to be with. Think about it—if you are with people who are apathetic and don't care about themselves or anything, are they as much fun to be with as a person who is busy doing things and who shows an interest in you?

Second, you get no points in our society just for being handicapped. There are few bonuses, and it's a struggle that isn't always fun or exciting. But you can set and achieve goals despite having a handicap. You must fight for acceptance—it is rarely offered as a matter of course.

The process of effecting change is often difficult. Changes in society come about slowly, like setting up services for the handicapped or changing our political system. If you are trying to change yourself, this also takes time and mechanical effort. Changing yourself can take a long time because it took years to form the values and ideals you are trying to change.

People who seem to be the best adjusted are those with a

good sense of humor in addition to everything else. It is not always easy to laugh at ourselves, but it helps. People tend to warm toward other people who can laugh and say, "Boy, I really messed that up!" or "Wow, I seem to have two left feet today." Having a sense of humor doesn't necessarily mean only being funny and cracking jokes, but also being responsive to humorous situations that exist in all aspects of life.

3

Ideas That Restrict Our Lives

by Ruth Wessler

Practically all of us could live fuller, freer lives. Many things interfere with our freedom. To a greater or lesser extent our bodies restrict us in activities that might bring us satisfaction. To a greater or lesser extent other people and the society around us will restrict us from doing things we might enjoy. These restrictions and limitations are there—they are real, and may not be subject to change. But for most of us, by far the greatest source of restriction is one we *can* change—we can change our thoughts and ideas.

How do thoughts and ideas restrict? Consider the European sailors who believed the world was flat. That idea created fear when they strayed too far from shore. That fear kept them hugging the coastlines as they sailed around Africa to the East Indies. Columbus, who also believed the earth was flat, gradually changed his belief on the basis of logs and charts he carefully studied. Coming to believe that there was no edge of the earth from which he would plunge reduced his fear of sailing into uncharted waters and led to his freedom to do so. Of course, Columbus did not just change his mind and sail off into the sunset. He spent years trying to convince others that he was correct. Then, once he found someone to support his voyage, he had to convince sailors to join his crews. We, of course, know the end of this story which well illustrates how ideas, strongly held, strongly influence the history of mankind.

Ideas, strongly held, also strongly influence our personal histories. We as individuals carry with us ideas and beliefs that keep us hugging our personal coastlines, keep us from exploring uncharted waters—ideas that restrict our lives.

The restricting ideas are those that lead to fear or anxiety. The human response to fear or anxiety is to avoid it like the plague. Thus if I believe that it would be awful or dangerous in some way to fail, to do poorly at some task (a common idea), in order to avoid the anxiety created by this idea I may never compete, never try, or try only when I feel fairly sure of succeeding. Not trying, I won't fail. Not failing, I won't feel so bad. But I also may be avoiding a great many activities I could enjoy if I were not so fearful of failing, of not doing well.

Another common idea is that it is awful to be disapproved by others. This idea leads to fear of not pleasing others, of saying the "wrong" thing. Holding this idea can be very restricting for us in our dealing with others, be they close to us like parents or friends, or sometimes even perfect strangers. It restricts us in expressing our true feelings, especially when we are annoyed or bothered by the other person's actions. It restricts us in reaching out to others, taking the initiative in social relationships—for what if I'm turned down? It keeps us waiting for others to reach out to us, sometimes a long wait.

Restricting ideas—ideas that cause undue fear or anxiety— have several elements in common. Let us examine these elements to see how we can change our ideas, to think differently. The two basic components of restricting ideas are "awfulizing" and "demandingness." The first, awfulizing, means that we are anticipating, believing that something awful is going to happen. If we believe that something is awful or going to be awful, we are going to experience feelings that fit with that belief—fear, anxiety, perhaps depression and shame. Perhaps you have said to yourself, "Wouldn't that be terrible," about something. And how did you feel? If you have been very uptight about taking a test, for instance, weren't you thinking something like, "Wouldn't it be awful (terrible) if I didn't know the answers, if I blocked and couldn't think?" *That* is awfulizing. The unfortunate aspect of awfulizing is that it tends to create upsetting feelings, like anxiety, that make it even more difficult, sometimes impossible, to achieve what we want to do in the first place. Believing that it is awful to fail makes it doubly hard to succeed.

Awful. What a powerful word. And how it determines our feelings and behavior. What does it really mean? Nothing could be worse than awful. We don't say that one thing is "awfuller" than another—worse, perhaps, but not awfuller. So when we tell ourselves that failing a test or being snubbed by a friend is awful, we are telling ourselves that that is absolutely the worst thing that could happen to us. Is it? For myself, I can think of many things that would be much worse. Like being slowly eaten to death by a swarm of ants! Albert Ellis points out that even that would not be awful. It could be worse—the ants could take even longer. One way to overcome this tendency to awfulize would be to ask yourself what could be worse. That will allow you to put some perspective on the situation that is bothering you. For instance, a young man was telling me recently how awful it would be if he were to be rejected by the girl he was dating. When I asked him if it would be worse if he lost a leg, he answered yes. He paused and then added, "You know, it would be worse simply if my car broke down." So in reality for this young man, getting rejected by his girl would not be good, but no worse than car trouble.

Now why do most of us have this tendency to think that certain happenings (usually failure or rejection) would be awful? What is awful to most of us is a threat to our self-esteem, our self-worth, our whole existence and value as a person. It is the threat against our self-worth, or for our more pessimistic friends, the potential confirmation of our lack of worth, that is awful. More to the point, if certain things do not take place (like being accepted or successful), *I* would be awful, worthless. That is exceedingly hard to take.

But if our worth as a human being were never on the line, never tied to the way we behave or how others view us, then there would be *no threat*. The problem is that most of us have ideas that do tie our self-worth to our behavior and others' reactions to it. Life then becomes a test. Not just a test of how successful we may be in a given pursuit or of how acceptable we may be to others—but a test of our human value or worth. No one wants to flunk that test.

Fortunately, such a test exists only in our minds. We can change our minds.

What exists in our minds, of course, is ideas. In this case ideas of self-worth. The two most prominent ideas° that people hold about their worth are:

1. I must be loved and approved by all important persons in my life or I am worthless, no good, a schmuck. Thus, if one wants to feel he is worthwhile, he mustn't do anything to provoke disapproval. Like saying the "wrong" thing. Like disagreeing with others.

2. I must be successful, never be in error, in whatever I do, or

---

° See Albert Ellis and Robert Harper, *A Guide to Rational Living* (Englewood Cliffs, N.J.: Prentice-Hall, 1975).

I am worthless, no good, a louse. Thus, making mistakes or not doing well in some pursuit means not just that you have made a mistake or not done well, but that *you* are a *failure*, an inferior being.

Consider the emotional effects of such beliefs. And then consider that they are not sensible. Not sensible in terms of cause and effect. Does it really make sense that lack of approval *makes* you a crumb? Do failure or mistakes really *make* you worthless? Where is the evidence that that is true? These beliefs are fine definitions if one likes definitions. Perhaps one day Webster will include under the word "crumb": *noun: a person who is not always approved and who makes mistakes*. But perhaps we could find that definition elsewhere, under "human": *noun: person who is not always approved and who makes mistakes*.

We will return to this important issue of worth or self-esteem, but first let's consider the second aspect of restricting ideas— demandingness. When we are feeling tense or anxious in a situation (say, applying for a job), it is our own demandingness that puts on the pressure, not the situation. The situation makes no demands. Even if other people make demands upon us, we may or may not do what they want, but the real pressure we may feel comes from our own demands to meet the demands of others. Thus, a test you may be taking doesn't say, "You *must* do well. You *have to* pass me." At least I haven't heard one say so. We do the talking: "I have to . . . I must . . . I need . . . I should . . ."—demands each and every one. These demands, of course, go back to the awfulizing—"I have to, because it would be awful." "If I don't, *I* would be awful."

Consider the difference between saying (believing), "I *must* make a good impression on this interviewer. If I don't it would be awful!" versus, "I sure would like to make a good impression, it would help my chances of getting the job. But if I don't, that's too bad." Believing the first will inevitably lead to anxiety and actually make it more difficult to do what you want to do—make a good impression. In the second case, you would be careful and feel concerned because you do want the job. But if for some reason you did not make a good impression, you would feel disappointed, though not devastated, because you didn't accomplish what you wanted.

If you wanted the job and didn't get it, you would feel disappointed. If on top of that you believed you needed the job or had to have it, you'd feel really down—perhaps hurt and depressed. This illustrates the fact that if a person gave up thinking that certain conditions were *necessary* (other than food, water, etc., necessary for life, not worth) that person would still *feel*, but feel differently. Many times when discussing these ideas a person will ask me, "But if I give up my demands, won't I then not care about what happens to me?" To which I (typical psychologist responding with a question) answer, "Why wouldn't you care? Don't you want certain things in life for yourself? Don't you prefer certain situations to others? If you really gave up the idea that you *needed* approval (for your worth), don't you think that in many instances you would still *want* to be approved rather than disapproved?"

A great many human emotions come about because we do care. When we are able to get what we want or desire, we feel happy, pleased, satisfied. When we are unable to get what we want or things happen that we don't like, we feel sad, disappointed, frustrated, annoyed. We feel these emotions along with others to varying degrees, depending upon how strongly we want or do not want something. The self-defeating emotions that tend to restrict our lives—anxiety, hurt, depression, shame, guilt—come only from either the possibility or the actual event of not getting or doing what we believe we *must* get or do.

The ideas that create these emotions are self-defeating because the pressure we put on ourselves by demanding that we do well or be approved makes it doubly hard to get what we want—to do well or be approved—because we are so anxious. They are restricting because very few people who believe that they are failures if they fail, or no good if they are disapproved, are very often going to risk failure or disapproval—the risk is too great.

Let's look at how to get out of this bind, how to change these self-defeating and restricting beliefs. To summarize, these ideas have two major components, awfulizing and demandingness. Both components are reflections that we believe that our worth as humans is dependent on either or both how well we are doing or how well others think of us. Thus, we *must* be approved. It would be *awful* if we weren't, for that would mean that *we were no good.*

What a dumb idea. (The *idea* is dumb, not the person who holds it.) What it implies is that my worth or any individual's worth can bounce around like a yoyo. If I'm approved (or do well), then I'm a great person, have lots of value. But if I'm disapproved (or have done poorly), I'm no good, have no value. Does it really make sense that on some days you are more worthwhile than on others? If you walked into the room where I am typing this right now, how am I to know whether you have value or not? Did a friend or lover just reject you? Did you just fail an important test? Did you pass it? There you are standing there. How should I know if you have value today? Obviously, I can't. Not based on a yoyo scale where your value can soar or dip. It seems to me much more sensible not to concern myself with either your value or my value as a person. Why label (or define) our self-worth as what might be desirable for us?

It probably would be desirable to be approved by people important to us. There are obvious benefits. But does their lack of approval mean we are worthless, or might it mean that they do not like some of our *behaviors* or *traits?* Whether they know it or not, it means the latter. You probably would want to, and it certainly would be desirable to, do well on your job. But does doing poorly really mean that you are no good as a person, or might it mean that you were distracted at the time, not as informed about the situation as you could have been, or simply forgetful—all behaviors or traits. Even if you are a poor organizer, for example, does not that mean that you are a person who organizes poorly, not a poor person because you organize poorly?

Well, you might agree, that makes sense. But how can I maintain self-esteem or feel worthwhile if I don't base my worth on something like approval or success? My answer is that you can't—unless you want to assume that all human beings, fallible as we are, have intrinsic worth that can't be added to or taken away. That might work for the more philosophical among us, but often is not useful. I would ask, "Why is it necessary to feel worthwhile?" (A question most of us don't consider.) Unless you are a philosopher, the feeling of being worthwhile is very transitory, the opposite of feeling worthless, when we are fortunate enough to have everything going well for us in our lives. But soon we either make a mistake or start asking ourselves, "Wow, everything is great right now but what if I make a mistake?" or "What if so-and-so really doesn't like me?" "What if" questions we seldom answer, but the answer usually implied is that it would be awful, terrible. So the great feeling never lasts.

The feelings and attitudes that surround self-acceptance, acceptance of oneself with all of one's failings and foibles, are much more lasting, much more in our interest, than feeling worthwhile. We can judge the worth of many things depending on what values we hold. Is gasoline worth eighty cents a gallon? Is it better to refrain from violence? Is equal rights a worthy goal? But how can we legitimately ask whether the person who does better in school, for example, has an A average, is a better person, worth more than the "poorer" student with a C average? I submit we can't. The student who has C grades may have more friends, have or earn more money. But then, is he worth more? Certainly not. Though it is legitimate to judge (as best we can) a person's behaviors or traits, how is it legitimate to use the same yardstick or tape measure used to judge these behaviors or traits and say that is a measure of the person's worth. The old saying tells us not to judge a book by its cover, but that's exactly what we tend to do with ourselves.

Go ahead and judge and evaluate your behaviors and other aspects of yourself. If you don't like some of them, work at changing what you can. Whatever you can't change, you still may not like, but you might as well accept the fact you can't change certain aspects of yourself, and, most important, accept yourself. Try not to rate or judge *you*. If you are having difficulties in school, for instance, you might *want* to do better (because of advantages in terms of jobs, further education, and so on), and you would do well to accept the fact that you are not doing well in school, a behavior you don't like and want to change. But if you *have* to do better in school in order to be a better person, you've just added a great burden for yourself.

I hope I have given you food for thought, for the way to begin to give up restricting ideas, such as my worth as a person can be judged by whether I am approved or not, is to think, think, and think. We carry around these ideas simply because we have been taught them. We accept them because practically everyone else also seems to believe them. But we seldom if ever think about them. Are they true? Am I really worthless if I am rejected? Does that make sense? Do I really *have* to do well? Would it in fact be *awful* if that attractive stranger was not interested in me? Is it really true? Columbus did not change his mind about the shape of the earth overnight, but he thought and thought some more about the evidence and eventually said to himself something like, "Hey, I don't think it's true that the world is flat even if practically everyone else says so." (My version of history—good luck with your personal history.)

4

*Preparing Yourself
for the World of Work*

Do things that build a sense of preparedness. A high school diploma is virtually essential for most good jobs. Apply for your Social Security number and open a bank account. Learn how to balance a checking account and file your own income tax return. Establish a credit rating early if you can and keep your slate clean. Register to vote. These are all part of the adult working world you are entering.

As a young person with a handicap looking for a job, you may encounter maddening discrimination and prejudice, architectural barriers and other obstacles too numerous to list here. Yet, an overriding consideration may be how you present yourself in the job interview or in meeting a prospective employer. Confidence in yourself and self-acceptance will be more important in the end than any handicap you have. You may be highly qualified for a job, but if the employer doesn't like your personality your chances of being hired are slim.

The characteristics we have found to be most important are savoir faire, a warm smile and handshake, looking the person in the eye, and a willingness to communicate and ask questions. Always take a keen interest in the employer and in his business, even if you aren't that enthusiastic at first. There's no harm in faking a little interest, since it gives you a chance to see if you really like the work after doing it for a while.

Be candid about the nature of your handicap, in effect saying "I can understand you are concerned about my handicap, but let me tell you what my assets and limitations actually are." Don't be afraid to suggest minor adaptations or changes that would allow you to fill the position.

In all fairness to employers (and to add a note of realism), we should acknowledge that sometimes a nonhandicapped person is more capable of certain jobs than a person with a handicap. By the time you get around to looking for a job, you have probably lived with your disability long enough to know what your talents and limitations are. Common sense and experience should tell you to avoid the frustration and disappointment of applying for a job for which you aren't qualified. On the other hand, if you are capable and willing you should make an assertive effort to get the job.

For most young people, the initial transition from school to employment comes as a shock. Sometimes they received a good general education which didn't train them to do anything in particular. Leaving school often makes people a little insecure: while they were in school the routine was familiar and they didn't have to worry about next year, since they'd just be back in school again. Many people don't really know what they want to do when they leave school.

Perhaps spending some time at a hostel or halfway house for the handicapped would satisfy your need for social interaction and experience on either a temporary or permanent basis. They are a good initiation for people who aren't ready for total independence and who want more freedom than living at home allows. The concept of residential family rehabilitation centers is being explored in many communities and might be worthwhile for you to investigate.

The process of moving from school to employment can be buffered by summer jobs between school years. Once you've worked and experienced what it is like to work with other people, you'll be better prepared to offer your services to employers.

Many high schools and colleges offer cooperative education programs which alternate semesters of classwork with semesters of employment. Such programs are called work-study, field work, experience credit, community, or work internships. Their main purpose is to give the individual some realistic work experiences. It isn't unusual for people to continue working for these businesses or organizations once they graduate, or to meet people and make valuable contacts that lead to work elsewhere. Some schools and colleges sensitive to the needs of people with handicaps have postgraduate career training and placement. Some private schools such as Archway, Adams, Vanguard, and Summit specialize in vocational preparation.

You may decide that volunteer positions with social, community, or government agencies are worthwhile experiences. Though volunteers are generally paid no salary, you demonstrate a willingness to work and accumulate some skills at the same time. If you are unsure of what volunteer capacity you would like to serve in, check with a volunteer center. The centers often conduct interviews to determine interests and abilities, and provide placement in the agencies they serve.

Rehabilitation and workshop programs don't appeal to some people with handicaps. They may associate them with charity, a personal failure to find anything better, and a narrow existence too far apart from the mainstream of society. The fact is, workshops needn't be any more boring than another job. Any job can become a drag if a person has no leisure interests to balance the work, if he or she is doing something that doesn't suit his or her talents, or the atmosphere at work is less than congenial. Some workshops are mainly for mentally retarded youths and may not be an appropriate place for people who are more intelligent. But even here a transitional experience can be turned into a valuable resource by being helpful to the retarded. Conversely, there have been reciprocal instances where, for example, a retarded person has helped a person in a wheelchair get around.

Before taking any job, find out as much as possible about what it involves. Some things to be alert to are: provisions for overtime pay, benefits (such as health care, pension plans, and vacation pay), the schedule of promotions and raises, possible occupational hazards such as dangerous machinery, and whether or not employees already hired seem to be happy there. A job that pays well may not be as good a deal as another position that pays less but offers you more in the other areas. So few people who are not handicapped achieve job satisfaction that one needs to consider a variety of factors before a selection is made. If you have any doubts about this, read *Working* by Studs Terkel.

Of course, few job situations are ideal. Some parents raise their children to inherit the family business, yet the kids may discover when they get older that they aren't interested in that. Some people work under subsidized employment. While you are working for a store or company, your salary or part of it is paid by your parents or an agency until you are skilled enough for the employer to want to pay you himself. There's nothing wrong with this either, but again, not everyone would accept the situation. The main thing is to be able to get the experience and to say on the next job application that you have acquired a certain set of skills.

In almost any community you could probably find people skilled in various arts and crafts, trades and skills who would be glad to apprentice you and teach you what they know. Perhaps retired citizens would have more free time and energy to devote to teaching you. Unions and businesses have in fact cooperated in offering training to people with handicaps. Service organizations such as the Women's Clubs, Y's, Kiwanis, Lions, Rotary, Knights of Columbus, Masons, Jaycees, and Junior Leagues have done excellent rehabilitative and recreational work with the handicapped.

Fellow employees can be a great help once you are hired. Some companies have a buddy system, where an experienced employee will initiate you into your new job and environment, introduce you to people, and show you where things are. If there are no formal provisions for this, you might be able to suggest it on your own. There is almost always a congenial employee who would be happy to help you learn the ropes.

At practically every job you work, there will probably be at least one person who will be unkind, make nasty remarks, and make your job generally more difficult and miserable, if you allow it. Responding to negative attitudes and insults with similar feelings rarely helps the situation. If, however, you are able to tolerate most of the wisecracks and laugh them off, while pleasantly trying to gain friendships, your good nature will be well received (except by perhaps the most stalwart of bigots). In some cases you may want to say in a direct way, "I would appreciate it if you wouldn't make fun of me" and then ignore further insults.

Going into business for yourself may provide good opportunities for satisfying work. Just a few examples are opening your own store, making things and selling them to other stores (baked goods, arts and crafts, clothing), raising plants for sale, being a freelance writer or musician, and operating a café or coffeehouse. Starting a business usually requires an original investment of several thousand dollars or more, yet low-interest loans are available to people with handicaps for such purposes. (See Part V, "Resources.")

Self-employment generally offers the benefits of freedom from a boss's pressure, setting your own hours or time to work, dealing directly with the public in many instances, and creating your own job in a field that you enjoy. Drawbacks may include difficulty in selling what you have made or written, inadequate patronage of your store, no material benefits (such as health coverage or pension plans), and competition from similar operations.

The training necessary for self-employment or working for someone else is available in numerous places. Formal education at a high school, junior college, college, or university often provides the foundation for employment. In addition to other educational sources we've already mentioned, correspondence and extension courses are available for home study from many colleges, universities, and private companies. (See Chapter 23, "Work Opportunities"—and be cautious here! Some of the private companies especially have turned out to be fly-by-night operations.) For the most part, these courses offer an amazingly broad range of trades, skills, and academic subjects.

It is heartening to note that changes are gradually granting people with handicaps access to buildings and facilities as the public becomes aware of the problems involved. Some cities (e.g., Cleveland and Washington, D.C.) have begun installing sidewalk ramps at corners and have passed ordinances requiring that new buildings must provide the handicapped with unrestricted access. In some places public telephones, drinking fountains, and washroom sinks have been installed at a lower level and doorways have been widened. We might take a lesson from Tokyo, Japan, which has bells at busy intersections informing visually impaired people when it is safe to cross the street. Brattleboro, Vermont, does this too.

These trends should eventually end the disappointment of having to pass up a job you are qualified for because the building is unsurmountable. Transportation is also a big problem for many people with disabilities. Specially equipped vans and cars are now available with elevators, seats and hand controls, though for many the cost is too high. There are wheelchair services in some communities that provide transportation.

In the final analysis, the ability to inspire other people to have confidence in you is probably your greatest asset in finding a job. Perhaps that is the second step of first having faith in yourself, no matter how handicapping your handicap is.

5

More About Looking
for Work

by Charles Weening

A company in New York City talked to hundreds of employers to find out what they wanted when they were looking for someone to fill a job. These are the results of that survey:

1. Knowledge of the job
2. Motivation
3. Personality

Knowledge of the job does not always mean that you have already had special training to do a specific job. It often means "Can the person learn to do the job?"

By *motivation* the employer means "If I hire this person maybe he or she knows *how*, but will he or she really get busy and give me a good day's work?"

By *personality* the employer means "You may know how to

do the job and you are not lazy, but will you fit in with my other employees or will you be a troublemaker?"

Many studies have been conducted by people working with the handicapped to find out why they lose their jobs. Employers word the answer differently, but most often (over 80 percent of the time) it is a problem in the "personal area." It is for this reason that some people who have a handicap have to start in sheltered employment or try two or three jobs before they learn to work with their supervisors and fellow employees.

A second important reason why some people with handicaps lose their jobs is a low "work tolerance." Some people can't work for a whole day for physical or mental reasons. If this is true, it is a good idea to start with a part-time job or go to a sheltered workshop to build up a better work tolerance.

Did you know that nine out of ten jobs in business and industry are obtained through friends and relatives? The employer is very smart to do this. If you had a good job, would you ask your boss to hire someone who would goof up?

People who have a handicap are often their own worst enemies when they go for a job interview. You cannot go for an interview acting like a beaten dog. How can you convince an employer that you have *knowledge of the job* if you have not convinced yourself? One way to start is by listing *all* the things you have done of which you are proud. After you make the list, find the ones that have anything to do with the kind of job you want (these are the things that you should put on a résumé). Making this list will give you things to tell an employer to convince him that you are an able person.

If you never had a job, how can you convince an employer that you are not lazy and have good motivation? One way is to be on time for an interview. If he or she asks you to come back a second time, be sure to do it. If you are given a bunch of forms to fill out, do it with a smile. Also let the employer know how long and hard you have worked to prepare yourself for a job if you can work it into the interview.

As far as personality goes, you should get across the idea that you do not feel sorry for yourself all the time. You have to convince the employer that your physical or mental handicap does not stop you from getting along with other people. Letting the employer know of your spare-time activities with people who are not handicapped is one way to do this. Another way is to be able to talk frankly about your handicap. Don't talk about it so much, however, that you bore or embarrass people. Many people are uncomfortable in the presence of a person with a handicap. You can learn from others who have handicaps how they get people to forget the handicap and see the real you. Group counseling sessions are good for this purpose.

Some employers believe that hiring a handicapped person will make their insurance payments go up. This is not true. Insurance rates are based on experience. If employers have a lot of accidents in their business, the insurance is high. If they have few accidents, insurance will be low.

Many employers also believe that people with handicaps are absent a lot. The opposite is true. Experience has shown that employees with handicaps get to work when others give up (snow, bus strikes, and similar things).

Most of the tips in this section are true for all people who are looking for work. It's up to you. Can you convince yourself and an employer that you are a *person* who happens to have a handicap, and *not* a handicapped person?

6

What You Need to Know About Sex and Marriage

Every person needs to know about sexuality whether or not he or she has sexual relations, and no matter what lifestyle he or she chooses. The facts about sexual functioning and behavior help us to make responsible decisions about when and who we will have sex with and how we will live. These are our values. This is not going to be a chapter on physiology, reproduction, or sexual functioning. The reading list at the end of this book will provide you with ample resources if you are interested in the facts. We're going to talk about areas of personal concern and how you might be affected.

It is our firm belief that you are entitled to full responsible sexual expression. Many parents find it difficult to accept the normal sexual desires and impulses of their children who are handicapped. Yet, your sexual pleasures, fantasies, guilts, hang-ups, and responsibilities for behavior are similar to anyone else's. If you feel you can, it is a good idea for you to talk with your parents about questions or worries you have. However, sex is a delicate subject in most homes. Many parents were brought up to believe that they shouldn't tell their children anything about it. They are often afraid that their "informed" children will engage in sexual behavior when they are not ready for it. But we know that people act more maturely if they know the truth about themselves and others: Ignorance stimulates immature behavior, not facts.

When children become adolescents they are physically able to have sexual intercourse. They are then told by their parents and by society to wait, and often they agree because they do not feel ready themselves. Dating and getting to know others can be an exciting experience that may be confusing at times. Sometimes you may be more interested in others than they are in you (or the other way around). Especially in your teen years, you may feel unsure of yourself and awkward with the opposite sex.

It is pretty hard for most teenagers to feel relaxed on a date or simply in the company of the opposite sex (even though many teenagers pretend they are comfortable). Young people usually have far more experience in relating to members of their own sex. If you feel this way, you might find double dates and group activities are easier at first and give you a chance to learn how to relate better with peers. Whether they are school friends, workshop or job acquaintances, neighbors or whatever, these warm-up experiences can help reduce between-the-sexes tensions.

Part of this tension is worrying about saying the "right" thing and being clever, as well as being sexually attractive. Being with other people requires a certain degree of self-confidence, believing you are a good companion and interesting to be with. Yet, the physically handicapped in particular may worry that because of their brace, artificial limb, wheelchair, awkward body movements, speech, or whatever, that they must be unattractive.

As we stated in Chapter 1, there are certain things all people can and should do to keep in shape and looking nice. Beyond these, there is a psychology of feeling attractive. You have to realize that some people will find you unattractive, others won't care, and still others will think you are beautiful no matter what. When you love and care for someone, his or her physical appearance isn't nearly as important as "depth" and feelings.

If you feel good about yourself, you'll be the one who decides what shape your relationships with other people will take—will you be acquaintances, friends, close friends and confidants, lovers? And part of this will be deciding whether or not to have sex. Even though your parents and teachers probably tell you not to, it is up to you because in the final analysis, you have to make many important decisions about your life yourself. I usually advise young people (say, under eighteen) to wait, and there are some good reasons for this.

Most teenagers aren't emotionally prepared for the intimacy and involvement of sexual relations. They don't usually understand that first experiments in the sexual area are often unsatisfactory or downright lousy, and they conclude that they must be inadequate, frigid, homosexual, premature ejaculators, or other things they don't want to be. Since you may already be concerned about your mental or physical state, you may be more susceptible to emotional upset and the resulting insecurity and anxiety stemming from unsatisfactory or guilt-ridden sexual thoughts and experiences.

The whole area of premarital sex affects anyone who isn't married. If your religion teaches that you should save sex for marriage, that may become one of your values. Most of society used to condemn any sexual activity outside of marriage, but today many people feel that mature people should be allowed to make their own decisions. People who don't get married until they are older and people who never get married often believe they are entitled to satisfactory sexual experiences.

Serious problems can arise if your parents refuse to acknowledge your sexuality. Unfortunately, some people conclude that since one thing is "wrong" with a person, then everything else must be wrong as well. If this is the case, you'll have to protect yourself and struggle for your rights to self-expression. If you are old enough and mature enough to make responsible decisions, this might entail disobeying your parents' wishes. Some very immature people think they are mature and make some bad mistakes. Be honest with yourself—if you aren't ready for sex, relax. There will be plenty of time for sexual experiences if and when you feel ready for them.

No young person has ever asked my permission to have sex. But I have been asked if it is normal to wait. And I answer, "Of course it is. If you don't want to have sex, don't feel forced into it." But I also say to teenagers, "Look, if you're not going to listen to me, at least use birth control." I don't mean something unreliable like douching, rhythm, or withdrawal. The Pill, diaphragm, IUD, the combination of the condom for the man and foam for the woman, sterilization, and abstinence are the only reliable methods we have. Remember that teenage pregnancy is much more dangerous to the life of the mother and her baby than among more mature women.

A Few Facts You Should Know

Anyone who has sexual contacts with other people (whether heterosexual or homosexual) must be aware of the dangers of venereal disease (VD). VD is transmitted through sexual intercourse, oral sex, anal sex, and even open-mouthed kissing with an infected person. The two most common kinds of VD are syphilis and gonorrhea.

The first sign of syphilis in both men and women is the appearance of an open sore called a chancre (pronounced shanker) on or around the area of sexual contact. A woman must be cautious, since the chancre may develop in her vagina where she can't see it. You should go to a doctor or health clinic immediately, where you will be treated with an antibiotic (such as penicillin). If discovered early, syphilis is easily curable.

Gonorrhea is noticed in men by a burning sensation while urinating and a puslike discharge. Women may also notice these symptoms, but since up to 80 percent of women have no visible symptoms from gonorrhea, they should see a doctor if they suspect that their partner was infected.

The external symptoms for both syphilis and gonorrhea disappear after a while, but the disease is still in the body. If left untreated, they can cause terrible damage to the body.

If you are going to have sex with someone and you aren't sure if he or she has VD, the condom is very effective in preventing VD from spreading. Also, washing the genitals and urinating right after sex reduces the chances of infection. Finally, VD is spread only through sexual contact with an infected person. You almost never get it from toilet seats, doorknobs, dirty dishes, or any other nonperson thing. (To find out more about VD, see the reading list in Chapter 26.)

Most young people, both boys and girls, masturbate. It's a blessing that our society is finally accepting the idea that masturbation does not cause things like blindness, hairy palms, sterility, acne, and other blights. We are sure there is nothing wrong with it; it is a normal expression of sexuality at any age, provided it is voluntary, enjoyable, and done without guilt. Masturbation sometimes becomes a compulsion (when you can't help doing something) for people who have handicaps and who are also lonely, bored, or confined to home, bed, or wheelchair much of the time. You might masturbate, for example, because you have nothing else to do. If this is true for you, it's a good idea to start working on other interests and activities to occupy what might be for you slow-moving days and routines. Masturbation is a desirable sexual outlet, especially for those with no others, but you shouldn't let it become a burdensome habit. There is no harm in it no matter how frequently it is done, but once is too much if you don't like it.

Many young people have one or several homosexual experiences in their teen years. For them, this is a normal stage of discovering and exploring their sexuality. But since society and most parents think that homosexuality is sinful, young people often wind up feeling terribly guilty as a result of their homosexual encounter.

It is important to understand that all people have both homosexual and heterosexual impulses and it is not unusual to have homosexual thoughts and experiences. We define a homosexual as a person who, in his or her adult life, has and enjoys sexual relations mainly with members of his or her own sex. One or several homosexual experiences doesn't make a person homosexual, any more than one or several drinks makes a person an alcoholic. With this in mind, we hope that you won't worry that you are homosexual, since so many young people have these experiences as part of their normal growing-up process. When they become adults, most people choose a heterosexual lifestyle.

We believe, however, that the small percentage of people who choose to become homosexuals have every right to do so, and it may in fact be the appropriate lifestyle for them. Obviously, it is more difficult for a person to be homosexual than heterosexual in our society, and for this reason most homosexuals don't publicly acknowledge their sexual preference. What happens sexually between two consenting adults is strictly their own business.

Society has some pretty strong stereotypes of what males and females are supposed to do, and a person who doesn't follow these rules may be attacked for being unmasculine or unfeminine. For instance, a boy who enjoys knitting, cooking, and ballet and a girl who prefers auto mechanics, math, and competitive sports may unjustly be accused of being homosexual. Yet, we are beginning to make people aware that individuals should be guided by their own interests rather than worn-out sexist stereotypes. You shouldn't feel guilty or ashamed for wanting to do any acceptable activity or job.

Marriage enters the minds of most young people at some time or another. Many people who have handicaps get married and cope well with the situation. Others, just like any group of people, never wish to get married. Of course, some people who are handicapped want to get married but are afraid they won't find a mate. If you are thinking you'll never get married because of the nature of your handicap, I encourage you to see the film about a cerebral-palsied couple who fall in love and marry. It is called *Like Other People* and has some beautiful scenes which illustrate that an inability to find a mate isn't always related to a handicap but rather to personality and self-image problems.°

Feeling sorry for yourself and deciding in advance that "nobody could ever love me" makes this feeling a self-fulfilling prophecy: Nobody can love you unless you let them and unless you love yourself. Enjoy yourself with people instead of being paranoid and worrying about what they must think of you. In any case, personal preferences are important and no one should get married because everyone else seems to be doing it. More and more people are proving that the single life is a valid one.

Some parents insist as an absolute prerequisite that you be capable of financial independence before getting married. This is an important consideration—your parents may rightfully not

° Perennial Films, 1825 Willow Road, Northfield, Ill. 60093.

wish to support the marriage for years. If at least one partner is employable, this may not be a problem. Yet, if neither can work, but both parents planned on supporting their child anyway, sharing the expenses of providing for a couple instead of two individuals can be a wise decision and even save money. Marriage gives many handicapped a great feeling of independence as long as some agreeable arrangement can be worked out.

The success of a marriage certainly depends on more than adequate finances. It is very important for you to feel you are emotionally mature enough to deal with another person's problems and the problems you would share. This usually involves much responsibility and work: cleaning, dishes, repairs, shopping, laundry, cooking, etc., etc. Especially when you begin to live with someone, sharing these "little" things can become the focus of major disagreements. This also points out that much of married life is similar to unmarried life: unexciting routine. This may sound awfully pessimistic to you, but in light of the fact that roughly one-third of all marriages end in divorce, you should be careful and patient in making your decision.

Partners must be very sensitive to each other's sexual needs and desires, and should be understanding if special procedures must be followed: adjusting a catheter, removal of braces or artificial limbs, different positions for comfort. You may have to be more imaginative in your sexual affairs than the average person.

Our society and media have placed tremendous emphasis on the man-woman relationship, with sexual intercourse as the fullest expression of their sexuality. The implication is also that if you aren't enjoying frequent, intense orgasms, then you are hung up and unfulfilled.

The only rules for one's sexual expression are that it should be voluntary, enjoyable, and nonexploitative. Beyond this, individuals should be comfortable with whatever satisfies them.

If you are satisfied with sex once a month, then don't be

bothered by statistics that state the average couple has sex 2.3 times per week. If intercourse is difficult or impossible for you, but you enjoy other forms of physical closeness, this is all right too. Don't let anyone tell you that various positions and techniques are any better than others if you don't think so, that sex must last for a certain amount of time, that you must have an orgasm every time (or any time), or that oral and anal sex are perverse. Be guided by your own and by your partner's preferences.

If you are having sexual difficulty, such as premature ejaculation (coming immediately before or just after entry into the vagina), impotence (inability to achieve or sustain an erection or have an ejaculation), frigidity (no lubrication or enjoyment or orgasm from sex), then you might benefit from sex counseling.

There are a very few handicapped people who are incapable of virtually any sexual expression. Some handicapped individuals are indeed able to enjoy sex in some form, but have convinced themselves that they can't. If you think this describes you, consult your doctor, or talk with a trusted friend, minister, or parent. Things aren't likely to get better if you keep problems bottled up inside yourself.

If you aren't able to relate sexually to anyone, all you can do is look for other things to do and different ways of relating to people. You'll be constantly reminded of sex by television, advertisements, movies, friends, etc., and you'll feel awfully lonely and left out at times. It will be one of those very hurtful things in your life that you'll have to accept. It may seem cruel that you are denied this physical pleasure, but it should not stop you from developing intimate relationships with other people. Sex is not the most important aspect of most mature relationships.

People who marry should understand each other's feelings toward having children. For some, no reasons other than personal preferences exist in deciding whether or not to have children. For others, however, there are external considerations.

If only one spouse is realistically able to care for a child, then he or she must agree to assume full responsibility. In other situations, the work can be shared.

Children for people who have handicaps sometimes becomes an emotionally charged subject. You might want a child, but your doctors and parents may tell you the child might be handicapped and you couldn't care for him or her adequately. In any case, you should get the opinion of a genetic counselor before deciding to have children. This is the procedure that many adults are now following as a safeguard whether or not there is a history of handicaps in the family.

Many people get married with very romantic ideas of what it's like to have a baby. They imagine cuddling and feeding the infant, giving all their love, and raising a child to be healthy and intelligent. These are very worthwhile notions, but they are only half-truths. Children are a lot of work, a great expense, and emotionally demanding. You may wish at times that you'd never had a child (most parents wish this at some time or another). A good experiment to see how you relate to children and if you could provide adequate care is to do several weeks of volunteer work at a nursery or day-care center. A marriage counselor who is aware of problems that commonly arise between people can provide insight into your future as a spouse or parent.

Couples (or single individuals) who are certain they want no children should consider voluntary sterilization (vasectomy for the male, tubal ligation for the female). This is a permanent procedure which only rarely can be reversed.

An unplanned, unwanted pregnancy can entail exceptional problems. You may simply not be capable of enduring the rigors of pregnancy or caring for the child once born. In some cases, the birth of a severely handicapped individual is quite likely or at least a disturbing possibility. If you find yourself (or your girlfriend or wife) in this situation, abortion may be an alternative. In the context of moral and religious beliefs, the decision should be carefully considered. Keep in mind the question "Who will care for the child once born?" No one has the right to bring an unwanted child into this world.

Healthy sexual attitudes and expression are part of a good life. Not talking about sex and believing in myths about it create sexual problems. As you know more about your own sexuality, you will feel a lot better about yourself. Ignorance, not knowledge, stimulates inappropriate behavior.

7

The Effects of Prejudice and Ignorance Upon Physically Disabled Youth

by James P. Lynch with Angela Thompson*

Having a physical disability is *not* a tragedy. It becomes tragic only when the effects of social prejudice, ignorance, and misinformation about it have not been isolated, neutralized, and controlled.

If a person's actions, thoughts, and feelings are interpreted by society only in terms of his disability, then his physical limitation is turned into a tragedy. Such social blindness on the part of society recognizes one aspect of a person to the exclusion of all others. Thus it robs him of the inherent dignity and integrity that is his by right.

Today, the few disabled people who exercise meaningful leadership roles in our society are a distinct minority within a minority. They have not succumbed to the prejudice and

* This chapter is endorsed by Disabled in Action Ltd.

ignorance directed at the disabled by the American society. One example is the present medical director of a rehabilitation unit at a Long Island hospital. Paralyzed quadriplegically, he is able to meet all of the responsibilities that such a job entails.

Historically speaking, many people who contributed substantially to civilization had physical problems. Among these were Robert Louis Stevenson, who had tuberculosis; Charles Darwin, able to work only a few hours each day; Kant, in constant pain from gout and a shrunken chest; Goethe, who could remember only four weeks of well-being at the age of seventy-five; Beethoven, whose suffering included asthma, chronic indigestion, and deafness; Homer, who was blind; and of course, Helen Keller.

Despite the achievements by a few disabled people, there remain countless others with similar incapacities kept out of the mainstream of society by a strong wall of prejudice. This majority has been conditioned to accept the barren fruits of bias and ignorance without question.

Prejudice and ignorance form a deadly pair allowing the so-called normal individual to react only to the physical limitations of a person and judge the actions of a person in terms of those limitations. The cost to the nondisabled person is the diminishing of his outlook; the price paid by the victim is the denial of his potential. This potential includes heart, mind, spirit, and personality. Such denial lets an artificial atmosphere dominate reality—a reality reminding us that all things which civilized man is heir to are not just products of the body.

Every human being faces the basic challenge of realizing his or her potential. For the disabled child it entails the added responsibility of keeping his physical problems in perspective rather than allowing them to become the chief focus of his life. To do so, he must face a series of tests beginning in infancy and ending at death.

The first test is acceptance of the handicap by the parents of the child.

Should the parents accept the child as one with the same basic needs as those of other children, they pass the first test. Their acceptance of the disability as only one aspect of the child is tremendously important to his or her growth and self-esteem.

If, however, they interpret everything a child does in terms of disability, they are rejecting his humanity. This rejection causes self-hatred and self-rejection, dooming him to barrenness, pain, and existence rather than life.

In some cases, this may be due to guilt feelings fostered by certain religious sects. These beliefs see the disabled as "a chosen people of God" and visual symbol of punishment for moral infractions of the parents. Accordingly, the disabled should hold greater religious convictions than the rest of the congregation. Acceptance of this prejudice by the parents puts the child above and/or below other children, robbing him of dignity and thwarting normal development of personality.

Even organizations created expressly to benefit handicapped children are not immune to this "disability-is-a-tragedy" attitude. Some agencies, in their attempts to solicit funds, portray these children as being worthless until they are cured. This monstrous approach to fund raising is supposedly used to "help the disabled." A few organizations, such as the March of Dimes, have attempted upgrading their techniques but they remain in the minority.

The second test occurs when the child moves out of the parental orbit into the neighborhood. Here he meets other children who are curious about him.

Their questions about him are brought to their parents. If the parents' answers are prejudiced, these children will reflect that attitude and reject the disabled child.

Unfortunately, some of these attitudes are so strongly reinforced by society that they masquerade as social norms. In other words, the bigot does not realize his bigotry for what it is.

Thus, it really isn't surprising that the young disabled child goes through a social hell in his earliest years. At this time, his parents must be sensitive to his struggles but not drown him in overprotection. They have to watch him get hurt by cruelty and strengthen him to face it again. This challenge, met successfully by parents and child, makes for normal personality development.

The next test comes when the child is ready for school. Which type of school will he attend—a special (often inferior) school for the physically handicapped or a regular public school? It is important to realize that many *children with physical impairments can attend regular public school* with minor adjustments on the part of the public school system. Will he be allowed to go to the school which his brothers and sisters attend or a special school?

Unfortunately, many local public school officials are indifferent or outright antagonistic toward the disabled child. Using excuses like "a wheelchair is a fire hazard" or "suppose the elevator broke," they do their utmost to keep him out.

A recent incident of harassment in one school district went like this. A disabled child with a reading problem was brought to the school psychologist. Before speaking to him or conducting tests of any sort, she said to the mother, "I know what his problem is. He hasn't accepted his disability." Then she proceeded to praise a special school for the handicapped.

An appointment was made for the parents to visit the school. After the visit the parents decided they didn't want to send their child to a school that was segregated. When confronted later by the psychologist asking, "What other choice do you have?" they had the strength to stick to their decision. They realized that in a segregated school their child would learn to relate only to physically handicapped children in a falsely protective environment. Knowing that the world a child reaches after high school is one in which people with physical handicaps are a minority, they wanted a school where their child could develop social relationships with nondisabled children.

The special school also perpetuates prejudice among siblings of the child. Because he attends a special school and they do not, they feel that something must be socially wrong with him. Moreover, he usually has more homework and gets home much later than they do.

Of course, defenders of the special-school system say that the added school work and loss of home life is done to give the handicapped child more education than the "normal" child, for the adult world faced by the former is a hard one. According to this theory, the greater the disabled child's intelligence and education, the greater is his chance to achieve the same economic benefits that other people can achieve with less education and job skills. Many of its proponents are so indoctrinated with this philosophy that some special schools have only one month of vacation a year.

The philosophy is based upon a fallacy, for it ignores the fact that intelligence is distributed along a continuum—equally among the races, creeds, and disabilities. The physically handicapped do *not* have a monopoly on intelligence any more than do white people over black people. Furthermore, an acceptance of this philosophy assumes that the more intelligent disabled child will move ahead while those with average intelligence will be left behind or ignored. If followed to its ultimate conclusion, the majority of handicapped people with average intelligence are condemned to second-class citizenship for the rest of their lives. Such reasoning can only lead to division among handicapped people, pitting the few with high intelligence against the many with average intelligence for employment, housing, etc. It would pit handicapped people against each other, blinding both to the common enemy of prejudice attacking them both.

Test number four occurs when the child reaches high school age. At this age, all adolescents have to define themselves as men and women determining their goals in life. The physically disabled adolescent has the same task with the additional burden of deciding whether he will accept the negative social values or not.

It is at this age that he first becomes aware of pity. Pity, that disguised vice masquerading as a virtue, is often accompanied by oversolicitation from his peers and teachers. Pity has the effect of granting him a few special privileges (like leaving lunch early to get to the next class on time) at the price of being denied rights other students naturally assume (*real* participation in social affairs at school).

Another problem is one of pseudo-acceptance. Here he is intellectually equal in the classroom but inferior outside of it.

The third problem is that of being on a social pedestal. Regarded as being more intellectually endowed because of a limited body, he is expected to maintain better grades than the average student. The cost of being perceived in this way is the denial of himself as an emotional being, stereotyped as a supermind. If he does not live up to such a standard, the teacher may be shocked. If he moves out of this role, he faces opposition. To survive, he must rebel.

Finally, there is the outright problem of bigotry. Here he is rejected solely because of his handicap. Regardless of what he does to combat it, he will still not be perceived as a human being with dignity. The real test in high school is one of reaction. If he allows or is forced to let prejudice overwhelm him, he will begin to believe the negative stereotypes, thus rejecting himself and others as cripples.

As had been shown, the basic goal for one who is disabled is to view himself as a human being of worth and value.

Today, throughout the nation, there are literally millions of disabled people focusing only on their limitations. Many remain undereducated and socially backward. If cured physically, they would still be unemployable because of the damage already done to their hearts, spirits, and minds by society. This bias on the part of society begins with the norm that a physical disability is a tragedy. If the disabled person accepts the norm, he becomes bigoted against himself and exchanges life for barren existence.

Why haven't the disabled fought vigorously for their dignity? Why do so many of them appear apathetic and indifferent to their oppression? Part of the responsibility lies with them; the *major* responsibility lies with society at large. The physically disabled have not consciously chosen second-class citizenship but have been *conditioned* to accept negative stereotypes reinforced by society. These stereotypes said, "Work with us and you will get along fine. Accept the crumbs as a substitute for the bread of life and be grateful for it."

Disabled people have surrendered to this reasoning for too long. Today a new consciousness is developing—one realizing that the disabled person is a human being with the same drives and instincts as another despite a physical limitation. Recognition of this basic truth has led to a demand for life, not merely existence. An important aspect of this consciousness is an uncompromising attitude of accepting nothing short of full recognition of the humanity of the disabled. This new attitude has begun to translate itself into organized action by the disabled and others working toward this goal. Still in its infancy, each day sees the growth of its power and number of advocates.

We are now faced with the challenge of eradicating the disease of prejudice and ignorance which has victimized the disabled for generations. This challenge is offered both to the disabled and nondisabled alike, especially the youth. It has two main requirements. The first is to put great strength and energy into programs designed to liberate society from its stereotypes. The second is to make a firm commitment to young children with physical disabilities.

This commitment is critical, for unless the young physically handicapped are reached, the disabled will never achieve full human rights or first-class citizenship. So, we must consistently strive to reach the children, for with them lies the hope of the future.

If this challenge is met, then forty years from today there won't be a need for articles such as this one. On that day a child born with a physical handicap will be recognized by his parents, neighbors, schools, and social institutions as a child first. He will live in a world where a physical disability is an aspect of a person, part of his humanity but never the sum total of his person.

When that day arrives, the promise of the Declaration of Independence will be fulfilled. The promise of the right to life, liberty, and the pursuit of happiness for all men—regardless of race, religion, or physical disability.

8

Person to Person

by Sarah Jane Atwood

I wasn't encouraged to do many things as a child. I could do only the things my parents wanted me to do. I have no doubt that I could have done a great many more things than I did during my childhood if I had been allowed to. But my parents were often saying "No" to me. It is unfair to any child, particularly a handicapped child, to be told not to do things of which he or she is capable. Dr. W. B. Terhune, in *Emotional Problems and What to Do About Them*, says: "Never let your decision be based on pride, fear of failure, an exaggerated maternal instinct (mistakenly called love) or possessiveness, which are parental driving sentiments that are not constructive." A friend of mine who works at a cerebral palsy clinic says that they encourage the children to do things that the children want to do as well as things the staff wants them to do. It's true that love is discipline, but love is also the wisdom to know when to relax that discipline. So I would say to you parents, have the love to discipline your child well.

I used to be so mad at my parents because they forced me to learn to walk. I figured if they had left me in a wheelchair I would have had the gumption to get out of it in time. I forgot one little thing, however. My leg muscles would atrophy, or decrease in size. There is a certain amount of forcing you will have to put up with. If you and your parents are emotionally well-adjusted people to begin with, the emotional storms will be short-lived. I would advise you to do your utmost to walk or improve whatever handicap you have, because when I went to a cerebral palsy conference a few years ago I saw a good many people in wheelchairs who had only a grade school education because they couldn't get to school. They were bright enough, but there was no way for them to get into the school buildings.

Making Problems Fun

The other day I was on the bus with a cerebral-palsied girl who usually left her mouth slightly open. Was I ever glad that my mother had said "F-f-f-t-t-t" (short for flytrap) to me whenever she saw my mouth open. Then I would remember and shut my mouth. Now that's making things fun. She could have yelled, "Shut your mouth," which I would have resented. I would give this advice to those of you who drool. I am sure that "F-f-f-t-t-t" would also work for you. It would take only a little ingenuity on the part of the parent to adapt this to any situation involving the mouth or face, or other problems.

On Schools

There is a great deal to be said on each side of the controversy over whether handicapped children should go to special schools or public schools. I know one blind girl who says that she is very glad she didn't go to a school for the blind, where the corners are padded so that one can't get hurt. She says that going to a public school was a much better preparation for college as well as for making her way in the world. Nobody goes out of his way to pad corners for her when she is walking down the street. In another setting, handicapped children have their own two or three rooms on the third floor of a building. There is an elevator, so if they need anything from the so-called normal children or their teachers on the floors below, they can use the elevator and get it. This is like a school within a school. I believe that things like this are being done for our senior citizens, for example, having communities of them living with college students. This is as it should be. I am very much against segregation of the handicapped or the elderly. But when I went to school there was no such arrangement. It may be harder on handicapped young people to do so, but I would urge you to go to a regular public school. Probably you will be better off in the long run. You may form friendships that will stand you in good stead in later life. Oh, I know how cruel children can be. But then, so can adults. And I think that the earlier in life you learn how to handle this cruelty, the better off you will be.

Nonhandicapped Friends

If you do go to a school for handicapped youths, you will have a peer group, and if you don't, you probably won't have any close friends, at least to begin with. Many normal children don't want friends with handicaps. It may have been that it was because my parents never let me do the things that normal kids do that made the normal kids shy away from me. So I would advise you to try to dance and do things a normal kid would do. Anyway, dancing is good therapy.

It is my hope and prayer that you will have a kind and understanding friend to whom you can blow off steam. Even if you have understanding parents, they are usually too emotionally involved: They usually can't see the forest for the trees. So it can help to have a friend to sort of explain things to you. Even if he or she can't give you any actual help, they can always listen to you, and I have found that helps a great deal.

How You Think of Yourself

This is a good example of "spread." If your walking, your speech, and the speed of your hands are your only handicaps, don't go picking flaws in yourself in other areas of your life, such as your marks in school. My parents had no right to question everything I did, particularly after a panel of three doctors had pronounced me mentally all right after my illness. Since they had professional opinions that I was all right, why did they persist in thinking otherwise? Don't you see how insidious "spread" can be? People will try to make you feel inferior just because you have trouble with your walking or your speech. Don't let them. You are just as good as they are. It is amazing how many people there are in the world who think that just because one thing is wrong with you, you must be disabled in every way.

Another idea you will have to fight against is thinking that everyone else is better than you are. And you will find plenty of opportunities to think this, especially if you have to use back doors because of architectural barriers. People will make you feel this way because you can't get a job when you get out of high school or college. Heaven knows, discrimination is not your fault. It is the fault of other people. If you have really looked for a job, and have been turned down because of your handicap, what right have other people to think that they are better than you? You may think that you can fight discrimination like other people can. But the only place that you are protected is in the civil service law.

Don't Limit Yourself

Don't limit yourself. That is my advice not only to you handicapped teenagers but to any other young person as well. Who knows what the mind can do? If a person is determined enough he can do just about anything. Look at the stutterer, Demosthenes, who became a great orator by practicing with pebbles in his mouth over the roar of the waves. So don't limit yourself by saying "I can't." Other people may tell you you can't because of your handicap. You must not let that stop you. You can go as far in life as you imagine that you can. But you will have to discipline yourself. Other people will tell you that you *can*, and it's good to let them help you, because some people care. Believe this, because otherwise you might get a sour impression of all people and life itself.

Now I am speaking of self-discipline. A twelve-year-old boy used to come to my door and ask for a cup of tea. There was nothing physically wrong with him. He was just mentally retarded. He never picked up the teacup, but put his head down to drink out of it. Now I can understand him doing it for the first sip when the cup might be brimming over, but to do it after that didn't make sense. If his mother had not cared enough about him to teach him, why didn't he observe other people and do likewise? I know he could do it, for I once told him to pick up his cup. He did, but the moment my back was turned he started putting his head down to it again. Dr. Terhune comments: "The individual who has gradually learned self-control and self-discipline is more comfortable, more secure, more efficient, and happier than the unstable, undisciplined person who really hurts himself more than anyone else."

Once Daddy used such crude language to a favorite teacher of mine, it gave me the inclination to suicide. He had spoiled everything. I don't know if things like this will happen to you, but they might. Particularly if you think everybody is better than you are. Also it is apt to if you get as depressed as I did. Parents, be sure to give your child the freedom to say "I hate you" once in a while. I wish I had had that freedom! A handicapped teenager is bound to spend more time than the average teenager moping around the house or being sad because he or she doesn't look or act like the average teenager.

After High School

After spending my high school years in turmoil, I wanted to go looking for a job. But Daddy said, "You are going to college. I want you to have a handle on your name." (He was a social climber to end all social climbers.) This depressed me, and I wondered what hope there was for me. But I somehow had the self-discipline to smile and keep going. You have to be able to at least count on yourself.

Whether you go to college or not is your business. After high school or college you will go looking for a job. Forget the employment agencies. They take only the easy ones. Go pounding the pavements and be prepared to swallow all kinds of excuses. I once applied for a job in an apartment building office. The girl in the office got up from her desk when I entered, and while I was walking over to her desk I could see her eyes get bigger and bigger as she watched me walk across the floor. I could just see her deciding that the job was filled. I asked her anyway, though. When I came out I was quite

amused by the way her eyes had gotten so big, and I was vastly
relieved that I would not be working in that atmosphere.

Work

You may end up going to your State Rehabilitation Office.
They will have you apply at a sheltered workshop. That's what
they did with me. After due time you will be admitted. Some
people like it, others don't. You will go for nine weeks for
evaluation and then you may get double-crossed like I did and
have to go for twenty-six weeks more. After, they may want you
to stay there for years until they locate a job for you. It may be
that the word "handicap" will be in the Civil Rights Law by the
time you go job hunting. The only place the handicapped are
protected from discrimination now is in the civil service. So I
would advise you to take that exam. Everyplace else employers
are free to discriminate, and do they ever! Even if you do land a
job, you have one more hurdle to clear. New York State (and
others) has a permit for employers of handicapped persons so
that they can pay them less than the minimum hourly wage. I
once called the Department of Labor and asked how many
states had this permit. The clerk who answered said all of them
did. With all of these strikes against you, you might better stay
home. Or if you like, stay in a sheltered workshop all your life.
But I want to emphasize this point: If you stop looking for a job,
you are not necessarily a quitter—as long as you find something
to do. Write a book, or fight for more realistic laws for the
handicapped. You may be even better occupied than those
people with an eight-hour-a-day job.

Don't let it sink into your consciousness if anybody calls you a
quitter. There are many things as important as an eight-hour-a-
day job. And you have to be a "quitter" in some things so that
you will have time for more important things. Our social values

at this time (the mid-1970s) are so constructed that people look down their noses at you if you don't have a steady job, but they are missing something too.

So develop an immunity to slights and do what you think is really important. But don't think for one minute that I am advocating a life of idleness and just watching TV. You can't just sit there and let Social Security take care of you. Keep busy at something, even if it is only needlework or knitting. However, if you are bent, bound, and determined to get a job, keep this in mind: If you go to work and work for nine months, your disabled child Social Security benefits are revoked. If anything happens and you get disabled again it will be seven years before you get them back. This law is meant to help the handicapped, but does it not rob them of initiative?

Sex and Marriage

A child can tell when a parent is embarrassed. When I asked Mother about sex, she answered with reluctance and embarrassment. I didn't ask again. This was when I was in my early twenties. Anyway, my father had done all he could to keep me from marriage. However, when I was at the workshop, a girl in a wheelchair who worked there got married. I have seen blind people who got married and had children. I see no reason why you shouldn't marry, if you want. But as far as childbearing goes, I would ask your doctor if I were you.

A Thought About Faith

I know that what I am about to say now may seem like a paradox: Have faith in the goodness of God. So many parents and handicapped people are apt to blame God for doing this terrible thing to them. That is only one way of looking at it. It may be that God thought these two people were worthy of being trusted with one of His "special" children, a handicapped baby. If the parents really believe this, the child will grow up with an abiding faith in God. This is the best thing anyone, handicapped or not, can have to fit him or her for the vicissitudes of life.

9

One Way of Seeing Yourself

by Philip Schnipper

If one does not show respect for oneself why expect it from others?

I have found that people don't really like to be with me when I am complaining or asking for approval. They don't want to spend the time identifying with my problems. That puts a strain on the relationship. People like to be with people with whom they feel comfortable, from whom they can get as much help as they can give. Sharing has to be equal.

I have found that you cannot like anyone else if you don't like yourself first. The first thing one has to accomplish is to figure out what you like and don't like about yourself. I know it will be hard to be objective, but try. Make a list and in one column note your strengths and in another your weaknesses. I bet you will find what I found out: I have a lot more positive than negative aspects. This made me realize I at least had something going for me.

When you spend too much energy worrying about what you don't have, you won't have time to do or care about anything else.

Once you start to look at your "do's" instead of your "don'ts" you will realize that you are basically like everyone else. You should not worry about what other people say, for you now know what you have to offer. When you no longer need to have other people building you up, you will have time for others and will be making friends.

One who goes through life always saying "I don't care" ends up like a piece of clay—molded by other people to their likings instead of developing one's own potential. When you say "I don't care" to someone you are saying "I am yours, do what you wish with me." Perhaps you want to be accepted by other people so badly that you are afraid of making demands for fear that you will be ridiculed. Try to avoid that.

If you don't look out for yourself, who do you think is going to do it? Who knows you and your needs better than you? If you do not take a stand and say, "I *do* care what happens to me," people are going to step all over you.

You may be surprised that people like to be around people who stand their ground and who make their own decisions.

Major decisions should be thought about carefully, but one can be more spontaneous about minor things. A car should be bought only if one can afford it, but ice cream can be bought without giving it much thought.

Why assume anything?

When people say things that you assume are to hurt you, and you get angry, who is the one getting hurt? The answer is *you* are. The other person may have been upset and didn't mean it and you snapped back without ever asking why they said it or what was meant by it.

It is always good to talk things out with the person with whom you are having problems. The person may not even realize that what he is doing is upsetting you.

Suppose you ask a friend to go with you to a concert and he refuses, which makes you angry. You may feel that he refused because of your problem, when really he just didn't feel like going out that day. Don't assume anything that you don't know for sure.

The same thing is true in all relationships. When you assume too much, you risk hurting yourself as well as the people around you. Why not ask and find out why the person is acting that way?

He or she may say or do something which makes you mad, but you don't say anything and go home tearing your heart out. Your friend may not even know you are upset. He is having a good time and you are miserable.

Do yourself a favor and talk things out. It will save a lot of heartaches and aspirin.

Make it a policy to understand the person who makes derogatory remarks either to your face or behind your back. Getting angry with the person only makes him more willing to say more about you because you have given him a reason to call you names. If you fight back on the same level by calling names or ignoring the other person, you are just reaffirming his opinion of you.

The people who call you names usually feel inadequate. When a person has a good self-image he or she does not feel it necessary to put other people down. By feeling strong within yourself you need no reassurance that you are better than anyone else.

When you can look at a person in this manner I hope you will find, as I have found, that you no longer get angry but that you feel sorry for them. The handicap ironically falls the other way.

You have to ask yourself, "Who is really the handicapped person?"

Don't let a laugh get you down.

Have you ever had the feeling that people are laughing at you because of your problem? When I stutter in front of people I find some tend to snicker. I discovered after many years of observation that my stuttering really is funny sounding at times. When I repeat a sound like b-b-b-boy, it actually sounds funny. I understand that it is not nice to laugh at other people's problems and I am not trying to condone it. What I am trying to say is that people tend to laugh at other people's problems or accidents because they find the act funny. Take a good hard look at what *you* do when you are with people. See if you don't find some problems funny.

When people laugh at another's problem, they are not always doing it to ridicule or make fun, but they laugh because it looks funny; *you* interpret it as being derogatory. I found that when the people who had laughed at me knew that it really hurt me they no longer did it. They were not out to hurt me; they laughed at me as they would laugh at a clown or someone doing slapstick comedy.

It is important to realize that happiness cannot be achieved by anything external. So many people search far and wide for something to bring them happiness but end up dying unhappy. When you are happy with yourself, no matter what you have materially, you will be happy.

What I find helpful is to remember what I have going for me and what I feel I have against me. To my surprise, I usually discover that I have a lot going for me. I was really happy when I first realized this. I got depressed, sure, but those were the times when I only looked at what I didn't have.

If I am able to appreciate the people and things around me I feel good about myself. When some people look for good aspects of themselves, they often count only the things they can do, like playing basketball, sewing, or getting good grades. Yet one of the best things everyone can do is simply to be nice to other people, which is not a "thing" and cannot be measured.

If you are lonely look around you. Check to see if you are chained up, locked in a room, stuck in a hole. If not, and you can move and travel, check to see if maybe the loneliness is between your ears. Your feeling may be there because you choose it without even realizing it.

1. Try to make friends. Friendship is a two-way street: you must give it in order to receive it.

2. See if you make other people uncomfortable about your problem because you have not accepted it yourself.

3. Are you making an effort to overcome the psychological withdrawals due to your handicap? One cannot learn how to swim without ever going into the water. You cannot make friends by sitting in your room thinking about how bad your situation is.

Don't get upset if people don't call you to see how you are if you don't call others to check to see how they are. Your handicap should not be used as an excuse to get sympathy. People will give it to you once and that is the end of it. Other people without obvious handicaps have problems too.

Worrying is for one who has something to lose!

Do you find yourself shying away from people because you're afraid that they will reject you? If you do, ask yourself what you have to lose. If you go up to a person or group and you are rejected, you are not worse off than if you had not gone over to them at all. If you approach them and they accept you, you are that much better off. Actually, you have nothing to lose.

I know a lot of guys who have no physical handicaps who are afraid to ask girls out. The guys with problems have an even worse time because they think they are rejected because of their limitations. I know that no one likes to be rejected, but look at it another way: What do you gain by shying away? If you call up a girl and she refuses to date you, you are not worse off than if you had never asked. You do gain experience talking to other people. If she says she will go out with you, then you are better off than if you had not called.

If one does not show respect for oneself why expect it from others?

II

For Parents
and Families

10

A Parent's Concerns

I was recently scheduled to visit a family with a nineteen-year-old deaf and cerebral-palsied young man. The parents were a professional couple and their son was in high school. I remember feeling uncomfortable about making this visit because I felt it was going to be a tremendous drain on me to make conversation with this fellow who I heard could lip-read but was difficult to understand.

It didn't take but a few minutes for the young man to put me and everybody else at ease. The reason was the absolutely relaxed atmosphere and the general fun and sense of humor that prevailed in the household. After a few congenial hours in the home, the outstanding impression left with me was everyone's caring, nonpatronizing, enjoyable sense of humor. It freed any visitor, to say nothing of the people involved, from a constant sense of burden that a person with a serious handicap could generate if everything was taken seriously.

I remember telling them the story of when I spoke at a college for the deaf. At first I found few people understanding my humor, but then I switched to a different level of communication and the messages got across. Almost instantly, the young man insisted I retell some of the jokes that were not understood. It turned out that he understood because his lip-reading coupled with the fact of his integration into society allowed him to grasp the essence of my words. The whole day was a delightful experience.

It is not surprising that in some homes there is a heavy atmosphere where everything is foreboding and people stay away, while in others a sense of perspective and joyfulness prevails. I do want to stress, though, that there are ways of using humor that are patronizing and put-downs, while what I have described was enriching and mature.

It is a prime example of why people with even major handicaps should be integrated in the general world. It struck me how enormously important a sense of humor and acceptance are so that one can adjust and feel comfortable in a world which is not very sensitive to the interests and needs of people who have handicaps.

Now to some major concerns that parents of youth with handicaps experience. Parents who haven't felt or expressed some of the anxieties that this chapter will discuss are rare. Indeed, even parents of nonhandicapped children experience them when they compare their kids with those they consider to be more intelligent or successful. Yet, despite the generalizations we'll make, it must remain obvious that each situation is unique. The best way to deal with this material is to extract what has meaning for you. Similarly, we can't suggest that you must feel what we describe, or that it's unconscious or repressed; it may simply not apply.

Problems often arise, however, from our refusal to admit we harbor regrets or ill feelings. For instance, it has been our experience that most people have hostile and/or guilt feelings—not all, but most. Parents of handicapped youth must deal with thoughts and feelings they find unacceptable or damaging.

The birth of a handicapped child often causes parents to seriously doubt themselves and their worth as procreators and individuals. The man who sires healthy sons and daughters and the woman who bears them are traditionally considered virile, feminine, and a credit to the human race. Conversely, the parents of a handicapped child may feel inadequate and deeply hurt.

It is a tremendous blow to realize your child has a handicap. It can seem as if all your hopes and dreams have been ruined: Some people never recover from the unhappiness that results. Parents need and are entitled to a period of adjustment to their problems, which might include rejecting the child or each other, withdrawal, irrationality, uncontrollable anger, or depression. There is a certain art to understanding ourselves well enough to wind these emotions down and slowly build the determination to help the child with a handicap grow.

Many parents, when they are able to communicate deeply to spouses, admit to even having death wishes for their child. In meetings with groups of parents, the frustration, anger, and helplessness has sometimes exploded in admissions of tremendous guilt over these wishes. Once each parent hears others sharing their dark secrets, they muster the courage to share their feelings as well. A father once hoped his son would have an accident—fall down the stairs, get hit by a car. He urgently pleaded that he didn't really feel that way, but sometimes the thoughts crept into his mind anyway. Parents in the group nodded their heads in grateful agreement—they all were tremendously relieved to discover they weren't the only ones who had thoughts they considered "perverted." In the discussions that followed each group meeting, I revealed, much to some parents' surprise, that many handicapped youth experienced similar death wishes about themselves and their parents, and their resentment, frustration, and anxiety had created identical guilt-ridden feelings. Almost all of these people, parents and youth alike, said that their thoughts were sometimes obsessive, that is, they couldn't help having them.

I have some standard advice for people who feel this way. When we experience thoughts unacceptable to us—they may be bizarre sexual fantasies, suicidal impulses, death wishes—the overwhelming guilt they create insures that we will have those thoughts over and over again (guilt is the energy for the repetition of unacceptable thoughts). But it can help so much simply to realize that everyone has thoughts like these, that it's normal to have them. Obviously, there's a difference between thought and behavior. Living out some of these thoughts or fantasies would make headlines. Parents needlessly worry that their thoughts make them bad people, but since they still love their children and have far more good than bad thoughts for them, what's the problem? If you have done something to be guilty about, mature guilt will organize you and get you mobilized so it won't, or is not likely to, happen again. Irrational, immature guilt is not helpful and is, in fact, exhausting and disorganizing.

Another prevalent attitude is "why me?" Some people may accept the handicap as a message from God, but actually there is no rational explanation. If something obvious like disease, drug abuse, genetic impairment, or malnutrition interfered with pregnancy, partial reasons can sometimes be arrived at. Other parents torture themselves with self-recriminating doubts, searching for their own wrongdoing or indulgence that caused the tragedy. In any case, this is a waste of energy. Of course, just because someone advises you "don't worry!" doesn't mean you'll stop, but hopefully you'll come to understand that your helping efforts and resources are more important for your child than whatever caused the handicap. Though the worrisome thoughts are virtually inevitable, the question is, are they in workable bounds, can we get used to them and move on without becoming preoccupied, can they be handled in a way helpful to parent and child? One needs to develop a philosophy that says "I've been hurt enough—why compound the problem with others?"

Another troublesome thought is feeling guilty about having a good time. So many parents have revealed to me that at different times in their lives they don't like to go out to parties or anywhere and be obviously happy. It's as though they aren't entitled to have fun because they have a handicapped child. They feel peers in social situations must be thinking "How dare they have a good time when they have a handicapped kid at home?"

The fact is that you have an obligation to have fun, whether people understand it or not, and it is essential to be able to reveal to friends, relatives, spouses, and especially your own child that you are capable of enjoying life. Otherwise you will become a burden to everybody. Your child will suffer guilt for "depriving" you of opportunities for pleasure. Let me make an unequivocal statement I've yet to see challenged in practice: Parents capable of living their own life and enjoying it in addition to (or despite) having a child with a serious handicap enhance and facilitate the socialization and mental health of their child.

Closely related to guilt feelings are those attached to deeply felt needs for vacations, periods during the day you can be separated from your child—feelings not unlike those many parents hold for supposedly nonhandicapped children. These can be arranged in cooperation with relatives, babysitters, older children, friends, husbands and wives taking turns getting away, and the like. All human beings need time to themselves for hours, a day, weekends, and longer at a time. The assumption that nobody else can care for the child as well as you can is sheer masochism. While this may be true in very few cases, it is rarely if ever necessary for the child to be taken care of *all the time* as well as you do.

Sometimes there is a vague, uneasy feeling that you have to explain or excuse yourself and your son or daughter to everyone you meet. This arises from the fact that you often receive strange receptions or responses. Maybe people you thought were good friends begin to avoid you. A woman who gave birth to a Downs Syndrome (Mongoloid) child reported that her friends and colleagues seemed afraid of her, apparently because they didn't know what to say or how to approach her. Even her physician was afraid to tell her or prepare her for feelings of unhappiness. Her shock put her into such a depression she thought she was losing her mind. She said poignantly to me, "If only doctors would tell parents it is okay to feel miserable. That it isn't unusual to feel rejecting of the child until you can get over the shock and begin accepting the child. I began to think, if my own doctor can't handle this, how can I?" As a mother she felt wicked for not wanting to immediately hold and cuddle her baby. Yet, with some help this mother became devoted to her child and an active worker on behalf of retarded children.

Another reaction of people may be an oversolicitous "What can I do for you?" The best response, if you can muster up the courage, is to say, "Continue to be my friend, the way it has always been. If there's something special I'd like you to do for me, I'm sure I can count on you." Implied in this comment is the statement "Please don't feel sorry for me, because it isn't helpful. Be empathetic and understanding, but don't carry it to the extreme of pity, which I don't need and don't want."

It's a good idea, however, to educate your friends and relatives so they know what to expect. Acting as if nothing is different usually leaves people with little idea of how to relate to a person with a handicap. One of the worst things is to assume that other people won't understand or be sympathetic, and to avoid inviting friends to your home as the result. Point out the fact that although your child cannot participate in some activities, that his or her desires and feelings are just like anyone else's. Since some people who don't know any better tend to baby-talk to people with handicaps, encourage friends to be as intellectual as they please.

All of these fears and uncertainties are related to several important realities. One is a sense of deprivation, and awareness that the situation in most cases will never end. It is one thing to have a broken leg that will eventually heal, or to be near fatally ill and recover, but it is another matter to know your child will always be cerebral-palsied, brain-injured, and so on. Of course, a large number of people who have handicaps are productive, do marry and live autonomous lives. This is not often seen as likely by parents whose children are severely handicapped.

Implicit in all this is the overriding concern, "Am I doing the right thing?" A lot of stimuli point to "the way"; volumes of advice, the media, professionals who disagree, in-laws, the push to be over- or undersolicitous or protective—the whole scene. It is difficult to reach the optimum level of maturity, which is "I am doing the best I can."

In my view, the overriding consideration should be "What can best enhance the socialization of my children?" Much more important than their reading level, math ability, and general studies might be a relaxing game of cards or a conversation. On the other hand, there are many people with handicaps who could not have survived elementary and high school without the support of parents, or achieved confidence in college and vocational training and eventually employment. The point is that the "School of Hard Knocks," or one failure after another, more often leads to poor socialization and self-acceptance than a good learning experience. Each event needs to be seen in a larger context of how it might bolster the child's ego.

There may be times when it's important for your child to be with other handicapped people, for parents to arrange dates for them, to organize parties or social situations. Actually having the experience is more important than hoping an experience will happen by itself.

An area of concern seldom discussed is the stress a family member with a serious disability may place on a marriage. We have occasionally seen families where it has added strength and new spiritual dimensions. In these situations, husbands and wives accept the challenges involved, support each other, and think themselves blessed for what they've got. But more often, stress occurs.

Much of this is due to parents' failure to communicate what they think and feel and to ask for each other's support. It is not uncommon for one parent to believe the handicap is his own or the spouse's fault, as in the case where one parent wanted another child and the other wanted no more children. Or perhaps a hereditary factor in one parent's family history is suspect. Prenatal factors may be at dispute. In these and other instances parents may choose to withdraw altogether from each other or to argue a great deal. The tragedy is that blame can rarely be placed and is, of course, almost never helpful. It can only add to whatever strained relations already exist.

Often the mother has the main responsibility of caring for the handicapped child, although there are a few instances where the father fulfills this role. It is terribly important for fathers to develop a calculated interest (spontaneity might follow) in terms of putting aside a specific amount of time for being alone with his son or daughter. It doesn't matter what they do, nor should fathers feel pressured to do the usual ball-throwing or whatever. The main thing is not the amount of time, but rather the togetherness of father and child, and letting the mother count on some free time to get away and enjoy herself.

Whatever the cause of a dispute, try not to dismiss marriage counseling as an option. Some couples feel that overtly seeking help is an admission of failure. Yet, self-defeating attitudes like these are more of a burden than the truth-seeking experience of counseling. Some couples may find that groups for parents of the handicapped, organized to work out and discuss their problems with others in similar situations, are more helpful and less inhibiting than individual sessions.

We encourage parents to join organizations devoted to their interest. Do your share, give support, learn, and be an activist at least for a while. For some this may be a lifetime involvement. Don't feel guilty if you don't wish to immerse yourself in working for the handicapped on a long-term basis. Certainly not everyone or even most people can be expected to become continually involved to a point where it becomes their main and perhaps only interest.

In whatever organizations or schools you deal with, we favor advocating, whenever it is possible, the integration of a person with a handicap into life's mainstream. For numerous reasons this is likely to create fewer problems than segregation. In some instances, however, special and private schools or classes at or away from home could be just as appropriate for the handicapped as for the intellectually gifted and the affluent.

Professionals can be extremely helpful in our areas of concern, providing they do not operate on the assumption that they know everything. It is okay to shop around for the professional you feel most comfortable with, and who is caring and attentive, but not simply the one who gives you the answers you want to hear. Professionals who work for the benefit of individual clients and who don't systematically proceed from archaic generalizations often offer creative advice. Parent organizations with experiences in working with local professionals have valuable information about them.

In situations where the handicap is not obvious some parents refuse to believe their child is, for instance, brain-injured, and travel to perhaps a dozen specialists until they find one who will tell them their child is experiencing only a developmental lag. Although the initial diagnosis needn't necessarily become the basis for all future treatment (in fact, the best diagnosis can be made at the "end"), there is frustration and costly delay in denying that something is wrong. On the other hand, some parents think there is always something wrong and worry constantly, looking for signs of trouble and badgering the child to do something or stop doing something else.

This doesn't mean that parents should never criticize, correct, or say no to their children. If you wish you weren't so protective, the most effective approach is to try to eliminate the criticism gradually, one or a few things at a time. Deciding impulsively that "I'm going to stop all at once!" is bound for disappointment.

The other extreme of excessive praise also prevents a person from developing realistic priorities and judgment. From the beginning, parents may display undue affection for their child, who may grow up to feel that physical expressions are appropriate between casual acquaintances and possibly even strangers. Later on, parents may get into the habit of praising virtually everything their handicapped youth does, with the conviction that they are balancing the negative messages they receive elsewhere. Thus, every painting, assignment, or endeavor is called "wonderful" and there is no conception of what is really good. Constructive criticism is desirable also in that children will not be shocked when outsiders don't applaud everything they do. The model parents set by their own behavior, when and with whom they embrace and offer praise, is the best demonstration a person could have for forming individual standards.

Many parents spend a disproportionate amount of time with their handicapped children without feeling they are being unfair to the rest of the family. Make sure that siblings understand the time allowances. Often parents feel that their time and love are well balanced, only to discover through introspection or a hurt accusation that they have been doting on the family member who has a handicap without really being aware of it. It is okay to explain frankly to siblings that you must spend extra time with their handicapped brother or sister. Naturally, if your children understand that you love them no less and you aren't playing favorites, they still might not like it but at least they will understand and not feel insecure or threatened.

It is not always easy to consider the well-being and better interests of your handicapped youth. One course of action, say special schooling away from home, may seem easier in the context of daily chores and getting an education. But any service, regardless of its inherent value, must first be evaluated in terms of psychological preparedness. Your daughter, for instance, might need physical therapy for her legs, yet will have to first overcome her depression in realizing that the treatment will require years of effort.

There must be a carefully maintained balance between the needs of the handicapped person, parents, and a service's impact on the family. Some techniques are so exhausting to the whole family both financially and emotionally that even if the handicapped person benefits little, everyone has been harmed in the process, which may not have been worthwhile. For example, Doman-Delacato methods may have proven helpful to a few people and be worth trying for some, but for many families they have proven to be a failure.

A frequent dilemma parents face is being confronted with

gimmicks, remediation techniques, cure-alls, and so on. It is difficult to decide on what to try and what to reject. Much of what parents are encouraged to experiment with are materials issued by commercial enterprises seeking only their money. Yet, some of the methods are sincere efforts on the part of professionals to be helpful. The problem, of course, is knowing which to select.

Perhaps the best idea is to talk with satisfied customers, especially in parent groups, although everyone's situation differs somewhat. Almost any technique will work with 10 to 15 percent of the people who try it, but what will work with one won't necessarily work with another. The chances that a particular vitamin therapy, drug treatment, or visual training will change everything are unlikely; it may help, but certainly not everyone and not with all that's wrong.

Initially, one should be alert to obvious things such as appropriate diet, medical checkups, conferences with teachers and counselors. Though many techniques of remediation and rehabilitation are helpful, the important thing is not to see them as cure-alls. Sometimes unreadiness on the part of the handicapped person can make the most helpful techniques worthless.

There is also the question of whether or not a parent should intervene; guidance may be considered unwelcome interference and an invasion of privacy and independence. But it might also rescue your child from a difficult situation. For example, some handicapped person's main problem is clumsiness or obesity. If phys. ed. is the worst place the person could be, in terms of masculine or feminine self-image, it can be worth intervening and arranging for an excuse. While we basically support the idea that young people should be integrated into the mainstream, what do we do in the meantime? A chronic diet of failure, however much the activities are desirable, can hardly be enriching. A transitional period wherein parents arrange dates, social activities, interests, and appropriate pastimes for their children until they are self-sufficient can ease the anxiety that surrounds social situations.

This touches upon perhaps the worst problem many parents face—how to motivate an unmotivated teenager. They may reach a point where they don't want to do anything, are accustomed to only passive activities such as TV, isolation. That is why it is crucial sometimes to force issues you feel will be of benefit. "You are going shopping for clothes whether you like it or not," or "Dad is going to take you to dinner."

There are many advantages to creating opportunities for secluded experimentation: dinner out the first several times might be best with only one parent on an "off night," bowling at slow periods during the day. Relieved of the pressure to "perform" in public, a person's nervousness often gives way to his or her abilities. Yet, don't operate on the assumption that people with handicaps always know what is best or will simply open up under the right conditions.

Again, don't hesitate to arrange for relatives or friends to spend time with your child—other people are usually anxious to help and don't feel burdened at all. It is not unsurprising that there are still people who like to lend a hand and have a sense of doing good. Not all "Can I do anything to help?" questions are insincere or just in passing. Since they would welcome the opportunity, you could take them up on the offer of a ballgame, an afternoon, or a weekend.

Even something like television, which can be a big problem, has more than one solution. For instance, you might restrict the number of hours they can watch TV, with a bonus that they can watch any additional amount that the family watches together. You might then deliberately select educational programs (e.g., National Geographic, Jacques Cousteau specials, good movies, and documentaries) that will at least enhance the knowledge and interests of your child.

It is usually not helpful to point out how many handicapped

people have succeeded. Much more pertinent to consider is how similarly handicapped peers are coping. These much less spectacular successes may be more inspiring, since the great ones seem farfetched to most people. And though it's a cliché, knowing that you aren't alone, that others survive and perhaps transcend their disability, can be a comfort without becoming a big deal.

What of the youths who continually have their shortcomings pointed out? If teasing is a problem in your community or school, this is invariably the result of a poor administration in the school and bad manners in general, often through no fault of the person who has a handicap. It can be a good idea to make a direct appeal to the teasers and the school for a little compassion, an approach that would say "I would appreciate it if you wouldn't tease Mary because it makes her feel really bad" instead of an angry response of "Don't you know any better . . . have any manners?"

In attempting to resolve the strong feelings of your children, don't tell them stories you know aren't true. Lines like "You'll grow out of it, everybody likes you, we're all handicapped in some way or another," may be technically or obscurely true, but in the face of severe or permanently handicapping conditions such as muscular dystrophy, they are little comfort and not generally believed.

Your youngster will more likely believe you and will have a realistic perspective if your words reflect true sentiments. Comments like "We're not sure why it happened to you. It sure is unlucky. And it is harder for you to get things done than for other people. But that doesn't mean that you don't have to try or you don't have responsibilities," create no illusions.

These are also good opportunities to offer your support and understanding. If the child hears "I know you don't have any friends, but we care about you and this is something we'll help you with" they will very likely find it comforting.

It is another matter to encourage self-support, sociability, and interests on the basis of real abilities and desires. Whatever potential for independence is possible should not be smothered. Parents who discourage or prohibit their handicapped children from trying new activities risk reinforcing dependency, though it is often the child's hesitation that says no. The freedom to experiment is vital to discovering the personal hobbies, sports, games, employment goals, marital interests, and so on that develop. Without these, life's daily routine easily becomes monotonous. As we have suggested in Part I, there is a significant relationship between being bored and boring, between being angry and self-pitying and being isolated and remaining dependent.

Being an advocate for your own child entails abandoning the pessimistic attitude many parents have. They become so preoccupied with the problems and inabilities of their handicapped youth that they gloss over the successes and competencies. Take some time once in a while to reevaluate your teenagers' situation and progress and don't be afraid to perceive them in a different light. People sometimes confront each other with "We've just been walking past each other lately, not really seeing each other at all." The problem with our preconceptions is that they don't always let us see what's happening.

The abilities of your child needn't be conventional or seen as immediately practical. For instance, the chapter "Alternative Approaches for Teaching Mathematics" indicates that games such as Monopoly and Scrabble may be useful tools in learning math or reading, although for most people they remain leisure activities. If your child shows an interest in something you aren't absolutely positive is undesirable, don't cut off the enthusiasm. The seemingly worthless activity may prove useful or lead to something else, especially if the activity is initiated by your child.

Children are very perceptive of their parents' feelings and the handicapped youth is no exception. Your child may well know, for instance, that you were disappointed and depressed when he or she was born. They know that people relate to them differently and are hurt by it. Even if they understand why this is so, it does not diminish the pain. They want warmth and closeness with people and may be frustrated or outraged when it's not offered or returned. They may be consumed with feelings and confusing thoughts which parents are best able to understand.

Parents should assume the responsibility for communicating sex education and moral values to their children. Don't operate on the assumption that the less teenagers know, the more responsibly they will behave. Information and the trust with which it is conveyed encourage enlightened decisions among adolescents. It is essential to understand that people with handicaps have the same rights to sexual feelings and expressions as anyone else. We encourage parents to read my book *Let's Make Sex a Household Word* for practical guidance and information in this area.

Of course, parents know that optimal communication doesn't always happen easily. You may have to absorb a lot of insults, disobedience, and apparent hatred or disinterest before you reach your child. Since children are less likely to take the initiative and communicate, parents must often be selfless and reach out. If there was ever a time when you were overwhelmed with despair, and a person embraced you and said, "I understand," despite your stubbornness and withdrawal, then you have an idea of how your child may feel.

Parents need to be aware of the fact that teenagers who have handicaps are more likely to be negative and angry at them than at anybody else. People who suffer with handicaps tend to cause the closest people the worst grief, often because they are the only ones who will take it without retaliating. It's not a good position to be in, and a response of "Look, Mary, I know you are upset, but you are angry with the wrong person. Some pretty bad things have happened to you and we understand, but we can't allow it to affect us. Let's talk it out," helps place where the anger belongs. You might ask, "We wonder if that's really how you want our relationship to be." It's very important for parents not to take it personally and not to remain as the object of anger without letting their child know they are aware of his or her projected feelings.

You shouldn't accept all behavior on the premise that "he can't help it." Your child needs secure, realistic guidelines for the formation of values. It is important to be consistent. If staying up late and sleeping all day is all right one day but arbitrarily not the next, this is confusing. Similarly, any demands, threats, or promises based on your youth's behavior should be enforced. If you say, "If you continue to watch TV for more hours than we agreed upon, I will deprive you of watching it at all for a week," stick to it. Handicapped youth need standards, particularly in light of the fact that they are often criticized for behavior that would go unnoticed in unhandicapped peers. If your child is engaging in behavior you disapprove of, try what I call the one-sentence approach. Make a comment that reflects how you feel about it: "It makes me feel bad that you aren't able to keep your promise," or "I feel unhappy that you continue to watch so much TV," or whatever the problem is. The fact that it might stimulate some guilt is of no big consequence because guilt over doing something wrong can stimulate more appropriate behavior. Only irrational guilt is bad.

Once one is aware of some of these dilemmas and working toward solving them, there are some good rules to consider. Let me stress, however, that the kind of advice I give and the roles I suggest are goals, not rules you can follow easily. One way of looking at this is to ask yourself when was the last time someone told you "Don't worry" and you stopped, or you told your child to "Be good" and he was. They are worthwhile things to work toward, realizing that parents can't immediately realize their best intentions. It can take even longer to consider the advice of those you aren't sure you can trust or advice you suspect doesn't apply to your situation. These are judgments parents inevitably make for themselves.

11

Psychological Problems of Youth with Minimal Brain Dysfunction

A Special Section for the Parents of Adolescents or Young Adults Diagnosed as M.B.D. (Sometimes Referred to as Learning Disabled) *

The adolescent or young adult of our concern is popularly described as a person ". . . with learning disabilities due to minimal brain dysfunction . . . s/he has normal or potentially normal mental ability, adequate vision, adequate hearing and adequate coordination and emotional adjustment. To say it the other way, his basic problem is not mental retardation, poor vision, partial deafness, emotional illness or cerebral palsy, although these complications make the problem more difficult." †

* Revised from a chapter that originally appeared in *Learning Disabilities: Its Implications to a Responsible Society*, Doreen Kronick, ed. (San Rafael, Calif.: Academic Therapy Publications, 1974).

† *Learning Disabilities Due to Minimal Brain Dysfunction.* U.S. Department of Health, Education and Welfare, Washington, D.C., Public Health Service Publication #1646, 1968.

As I know these young people, they reveal areas of intellectual adequacy coexisting with areas of intellectual inadequacy. They may have other complicating problems—the most important of which is their tendency to be isolates (in other words, they have no friends), and they have a tendency to be unaware of the impact they have on others (that is, they find it difficult to generalize from experience). Their problems *presumably* are due to *minimal* cerebral dysfunction, which often is complicated by medical, educational, and psychological mismanagement. (Operationally we define "presumably due to minimal cerebral dysfunction" to mean that diagnostic and clinical studies, both medical and psychological, reveal evidence of cerebral insult without resulting in mental retardation or psychosis.) The now-neglected, but pioneer work of Kurt Goldstein—especially his understanding of impairment of the capacity to *abstract* as a result of damage to the brain—probably offers the best "insights" about so-called brain-injured persons; or as they are now diagnosed, "learning disabilities due to minimal brain dysfunction."

Without meaning to belabor the complicated and unresolved issue of etiology, I should like now to address myself to the problems of growing up for adolescents or young adults who are isolates and who tend to become further isolated because of their inability to function successfully in the mainstream of adolescent or young adult activities.

Many of the characteristics of brain-injured children seem to disappear or to be considerably modified during adolescence. This includes their hyperactivity, perseveration, distractibility— but not their uneven intellectual functioning; and like everybody else, their "short attention span" now seems more a function of boredom or lack of motivation than a byproduct of the injury itself.

What emerges is that the psychological status of the adolescent is a far greater determining factor of adult "adjustment" than the nature or extent of the dysfunction. Indeed, this "adjustment" principle seems to hold for all but the most severe forms of handicapping conditions.

It is difficult to realize how much is learned during adolescence through interaction with peers. Isolates miss experiences with the opposite sex; a wide range of socialization behavior which can be categorized as "savoir faire" or "cool"; and most vitally, the self-assurance and ego strength that develop in the context of group acceptance.

In the early stages of working with groups of learning disabled young adults—even those who are not from economically and socially deprived families—glaring deficiencies emerge. If I may illustrate from one such group of ten young adults, ranging in age from eighteen to twenty-two: None had been on or could handle a "date," none felt comfortable in a restaurant. These young adults didn't know what "a la carte" meant or how much of a tip to leave. Only two could manage public transportation. They had no idea of how to secure advance tickets for the theater or how to use the yellow pages of the telephone directory. Some of these "deficiencies" may seem trivial, but if you multiply them by several hundred other "little" things, you will find a young person who is "out of it" and unrelated to his or her own environment.

Without the "corrective" experience from peers, many personality defects become firmly entrenched, and it is remarkable how impervious young people are to their parents' criticism.

As I think of the same group of ten young adults: Every comment one young man made was overelaborated to a point of distraction. No one could tolerate being with him for longer than a few minutes. One young woman constantly boasted. Virtually everything she said referred to her "expensive" clothing, how much money she earned, or how she was really "better off" than the others in the group. One good-looking bright young man "arranged" to be repeatedly rejected by promptly falling in love with any new girl close to his age who came his way. One fellow was "frank" about all his comments and used obscene language without discretion. One girl, with a speech defect, incorrectly assumed that no one could understand her.

The young persons referred to above were in a program sponsored by a State Rehabilitation Commission involving Friday night counseling sessions at which time a clinical psychologist and college student volunteers met with the young adults. The parents met separately with a social worker. It took between ten and fifteen sessions before it emerged as a viable socialization group. After the forty sponsored sessions, the parents and the youths decided to continue the group on their own. In retrospect one must know that all of the individuals involved were isolates with little prospect for satisfactory adult adjustment. The groups provided opportunities for new experiences. They became friends with each other and were to learn many things that they missed growing up as adolescents without friends. For example, they learned how to travel to a nearby big city. They learned many ideas for enjoying their leisure time. They were taught hobbies and games and ways of arranging their lives so that they became much more self-sufficient.

We made inroads on some of the serious limitations that had prevented some of them from becoming employed. While most of the members of the group had been erroneously classified as mentally retarded, no single member of the group was, in fact, mentally retarded. It became clear that psychological problems and lack of socialization skills were the main impediments to finding employment. For example, one young lady seemed to be making a great deal of progress and was apparently ready for employment until it was found that despite a high school diploma, she could not handle math at a first-grade level.

If I could make any generalizations about adolescents with

minimal brain dysfunction, I would not give high priorities to short attention span, hyperactivity, perceptual problems, learning disabilities, poor coordination, emotional lability or impulsivity. However, I would be prepared, on the basis of clinical experience with several hundred brain-injured adolescents and young adults, to suggest that virtually all have difficulty anticipating the impact their behavior has on others. Their greatest handicap seems to be their inability to generalize from experience.

This would seem to be due to the brain dysfunction which makes it difficult for them to shift from the concrete to abstract reasoning. It is true that I cannot offer adequate research to "prove" this point, but I will hold with the behavioral description and leave etiology as a concern for further exploration.

Thus, we often find the adolescent friendless, with odd mannerisms, inexperienced in the ways of the world, suffering from intense feelings of inferiority and with an enormous capacity for "nothing to do" in leisure time.

As I have suggested elsewhere, any child, handicapped or otherwise, who can function adequately in a regular class or recreational program should be given that opportunity. However, special programs, classes, and facilities of all kinds are *sound* for those children and adults who otherwise would not learn and be able to socialize at a level which is in harmony with human dignity.

I have yet to discover a single brain-injured person who, as a child or as an adolescent, profited from being exposed to frequent or constant rejection, criticism, and failure. They become the victims of the so-called school of hard knocks. Even worse are the victims whose difficulties are compounded by inappropriate school placement. I am referring especially to the many thousands of children who were falsely diagnosed as mentally retarded.

Children already suffering from feelings of inferiority because they are different or slow or not doing as well as their younger siblings do not profit from unfavorable experiences.

Permit me to say again that there are no substitutes for friends, things one can do well, a choice of things to do in one's leisure time and knowledge (self-awareness and the facts of life in the broadest sense). This seemingly prosaic message becomes the cardinal principle for contributing to feelings of well-being among people who are handicapped.

A "corrective" prototype is similar to what I have designated as a Personal Adjustment Training program (already described) of eight or nine adolescents who, friendless, became friends with each other; "talentless," began developing skills outside the context of competition; fearing ridicule or exclusion and feeling worthless soon began to vie for the privilege of hosting the weekly meetings.

The counseling sessions focused on these questions: What does it mean to be brain injured? How to meet people? How to spend free time? What are appropriate presents for various holidays? How to cope with anger? Sex information? The use of the phone (information, collect calls)? With the younger adolescents the relationship to the counselors was characterized by fun, but sometimes: "I'm sure you are not aware of it but you are talking too loud!" "I guess you forgot that it was inappropriate to use obscene language in mixed company?" "Say, Jim, I want to talk to you for a minute. Let's go where no one can hear us—Are you aware of how much you are criticizing Gill? I think it is making him feel bad." "Say, Tom, remember to go easy when you meet a new girl. Don't ask her to go steady with you the first time you meet her no matter how interested she seems to be in you."

This counseling experience provided an excellent training opportunity for a doctoral student in psychology who was able to observe the group leader in an actual situation; the result was that he was able to take over the leadership of the group with supervision. Three counselors who had been induced to work with these youths were now planning to enter this field after further professional training.

Among the activities for the youths which took place either on Saturday or Sunday were several trips to the theater and museums, eating out in restaurants, which involved learning how to order from a menu and knowing how to give correct tips, and shopping trips for the purpose of learning to spend money wisely. Perhaps the most valuable of the weekend activities were opportunities for teaching hobbies, crafts, and different ways of spending leisure time. Each member of the group hosted the weekend activity, thus providing each with an opportunity to learn how to organize a party and make plans for guests, including preparation of meals.

The feature of the program that seemed particularly outstanding related to grooming. It was impressive to observe a group of adolescents in a direct experience of following sequentially the steps involved in good grooming, including such things as being able to read the labels on bottles and to make distinctions between what represented appropriate and inappropriate dress. Another feature of the program was training the adolescents to prepare their own food and to have a sense of being able to become independent in this area. Also, the efforts to teach them how to make change with real money were very important.

This personal adjustment program proved to be a valuable preparation for isolated young people in entering the adult world. Counseling related to actual socialization experiences, group counseling for the parents, and medical management of those who were more seriously ill, plus the extra benefit of training additional people for this field, seems like an extremely good way to work with young people who are handicapped in general.

Undoubtedly, a valuable and indispensable feature of the entire program was the group counseling of the parents.

The agenda was a reduction of guilt to a point where, contrary to the "best" American tradition, we can encourage in some areas *appropriate* overprotection of handicapped children. It is extraordinary how some American women's and parents' magazines have brainwashed mothers so that they cannot follow their own natural inclinations about their children without guilt. The parents help each other with practical ideas that have worked for them; they receive solace for having to "go it alone" and guidance from the counselor who assists in identifying situations such as the appropriate time to "overprotect." A good case in point is the physical education programs in public schools. Often designed to "exclude" children, physical education or gym is particularly hard on the neurologically handicapped child. If a child is having a hard time in gym, parents should not hesitate to get a medical excuse.

Attendance was remarkable; only illness seemed to be a reason for absence. Only one parent of the group members did not attend. A wide range of subjects was discussed including discipline problems, work with the schools, and relationship to siblings. At first several members of the group were on the defensive, making known their resentment of talking about family matters or thinking that their children were more advanced than the others in the group. This disappeared about the ninth or tenth session and here again the group of parents became very interested in each other and loyal to the group. Many arranged for their children to meet with each other and the group extended itself into social areas in many cases. It is interesting that many of the parents had previously isolated themselves from their neighbors and potential friends because of guilt and uncertainties about how to manage their child.

To return now to the individual adolescent, there is no substitute for the knowledge which permits interaction with friends without embarrassment. This is especially true of sex information. In a sense, handicapped youth should be better informed than the average youngster so that he or she will not be caught off guard, made fun of, or considered (at best) naïve. As I have made clear in my book *Facts About Sex for Today's Youth*, it is essential that youth understand the language of the street as well as be fully informed about the emotional and reproductive aspects of sex.

In our society there are many problems if one delays the "special talk" on sex until a child is approaching adolescence. The limitations to such an approach are obvious. Boys insist that they know everything about sex. Girls are not willing to acknowledge that they are even interested in it. Needless to say, attitudes are already formed by the time a child approaches early adolescence.

If we are concerned with the psychological well-being of adolescents or young adults who are handicapped, there is also no substitute for knowing how to "do things." We, ourselves, have been surprised by how many supposedly ill-coordinated or severe learning disabled young people can learn in the context of a psychologically sound, noncompetitive setting. I specifically use the expression "psychologically sound" because many of the *blocks* to learning are psychological. We had difficulty teaching simple percentages to the Personal Adjustment Training group (in order to learn the art of tipping), but we had little problem teaching much more difficult concepts when we successfully taught them chess, Monopoly, and other games. One particular adolescent who was "hopeless" in all sports and who translated all complaints into a propensity for "nothing to do" became very busy shortly after he learned one sport well (swimming, taught individually by an expert). It is surprising how very poorly coordinated young people can be taught bowling if the initial instruction takes place when nobody else is around and when they understand the scoring.

Sometimes the best teacher is not the mother, father, or a sibling, but a young high school or college student, who prefers this way of earning extra money to babysitting. Such a young person can be a successful companion two or three days a week in the form of a homework helper and teacher of games. Young people who have been hopeless in baking, cooking, sewing, or knitting, become, for instance, adept bakers after their first success with a packaged, ready-to-make brownie mix.

Parents or teachers who have repeatedly failed in teaching certain skills should "give up" this role to a teenager or young college student with instruction that whatever is taught should be taught only when they are by themselves, indirectly if possible, most desirably as part of a game, and only after it is clear that they like each other.

New interests develop among adolescents when they discover, for the first time, how to watch and score spectator sports such as basketball, football, and others.

We have adhered to false notions of limiting experiences for neurologically handicapped young people when, as a matter of fact, we must find ways to broaden and expand their horizons. So many have been "turned off" from reading books and newspapers and from culture in general because of premature or negative exposure. Games and experiences with people they like are ways of "turning on" young people.

Youth with minimal brain dysfunction who can make friends (even if only among others similarly handicapped) and who have some talents and enjoy leisure-time activities, who are not naïve and are not preeminently self-depreciating, can "make it" as adults.

In other words, young people with handicaps who are reasonably well adjusted psychologically will function reasonably well as independent adults despite their handicap.

12

Commonly Asked Questions

Over the years, parents who have children with handicaps have asked me countless questions concerning their children's well-being. I have answered some of the most important ones here. These questions and answers originally appeared, in slightly different form, in a pamphlet entitled *On Being the Parent of a Handicapped Youth*, by Sol Gordon.*

Vocational Rehabilitation Agencies

Of the many places I've tried to secure help for my son, the rehabilitation commission of my state has given me the biggest

* New York Association for Brain Injured Children, 95 Madison Ave., New York, N.Y. 10016.

runaround. What's the story? Are there better places, or are there ways to get things accomplished with the commission that I don't know about?

My experience with the rehabilitation commissions I've encountered has been frustrating. This is especially true for parents of neurologically handicapped youth. Basically, before contacting any such governmental offices, it is best to be prepared.

Before you apply for assistance from your local vocational rehabilitation office, make it a point to thoroughly familiarize yourself with the law. Officials frequently stipulate age and other conditions for eligibility that are inaccurate.

Often a workable approach is to have a local, elected official make initial inquiries for you. Since there are even some state offices that spend most of their time dodging legitimate claims, it is surprising how much you can accomplish if you yourself understand the criteria for eligibility.

Unfortunately, as is often the case, parents wind up expending a lot of energy helping state programs for the handicapped do their own job. Obviously, there are notable exceptions to this generalization, but complaints about the state system are so widespread that it is imperative for parents to be alert to the problem and recourses to action.

Activities

I see normal children participating in activities common for their age group, but I am frequently unsure of what our son should be allowed to do. Can you give me some guidelines?

Judging beforehand what activities a youth who has a handicap would be capable of is a difficult matter. I think, though, that the youths should be permitted to experiment with

virtually anything socially acceptable that interests them, unless
it is clearly impossible because of their particular disability.
Further, if the person displays no interest in something (or
anything) at the start, parents should take the initiative and try
to stimulate their child's interest. This should not be done in a
manner which might create a feeling of undue pressure.

Since so many teenagers with handicaps have trouble making
and keeping friends, parents should seek to "team" their
children with other handicapped adolescents and introduce
them to varieties of organized social experiences. Such experiences as summer camp, clubs, or play groups can be nonthreat-
ening and provide relief from isolation. Competitive activities
should be avoided, to prevent too many negative experiences.
Most important, parents are warned not to discourage their
children's desires unless necessary. If they hear too often of the
things they can't do, they'll believe it applies to everything after
a while. If you are unsure, speak with professional counselors
and parents of similarly handicapped youth for their experience.

Concentrate on success. As your adolescent's confidence
grows, he or she will assume more responsibility for his or her
own affairs. Initial successes of buying one's own clothes or
getting around town may lead to more complex skills and a
sense of what one is capable of.

Television and Leisure-Time Activities

*My husband and I are concerned over the quantity of
television viewing our handicapped daughter does. We realize
that some may be valuable as a teaching aid, but wouldn't her
time be better spent doing something else?*

For handicapped youth with an excess of leisure time,
television often becomes the great time filler. Yet, excess TV

viewing promotes escapism from the world and its problems. Some TV is, of course, worthwhile, but should always be supplemented with more challenging activities.

People with handicaps are perhaps more likely to be affected by the violence, sexual emphasis, monotony, and anti-intellectualism they see on TV because, in general, they have fewer experiences and less interaction with others to discredit them. It is appropriate for parents to restrict the amount of time spent watching TV. They may find it advantageous to watch some educational programs and encourage their adolescent to watch with them, discussing the program as it goes along. Make it understood you limit TV time because it isn't healthy for them to remain fixated on the idiot box.

Reading may be difficult after an exhausting day at school, but magazines and comic books appeal to nearly everyone, though they should not be pushed. Everyone needs intellectual stimulation, and hobbies, games, and special interests are excellent cultural stimulants.

Physical activity is a must, and with the exception of a few severely physically handicapped, everyone is capable of some form of exercises, even if confined to a wheelchair. Parents should provide opportunities for body building and isometric exercises, and for noncompetitive sports. Swimming, Ping-Pong, billiards, bicycling, bowling, hiking, tennis, all are worthwhile if possible.° Spectator sports may be entertaining as well and are a good way to generate conversation with friends.

Automobiles

Our seventeen-year-old daughter has just reached the age of eligibility to drive a car in our state. Although she is well

---

° Naturally, you want to follow your doctor's orders.

coordinated, she has difficulty deciphering road signs and telling right from left. Should we allow her to get her license?

Every adolescent, regardless of whether she has a handicap or not, dreams of driving or owning a car. If she is able to master the skill and has at least normal reflexes and reaction time, driving bolsters self-confidence and reliance, and helps gain membership into teenage groups. I advise letting your daughter try to learn with the help of a driving instructor who is best qualified to judge if your daughter will make a competent driver. (It is usually better for the parent not to be the teacher.)

Psychotherapy?

My child's counselor at school recently recommended we take our handicapped son to a psychotherapist. Our child is physically disabled and we realize this creates corresponding psychological problems. We are willing to try anything, providing, of course, it is in our son's better interests.

Generally speaking, traditional forms of psychotherapy dealing with unconscious motivations of behavior are not helpful to youth who have difficulty handling abstract ideas. They are often confused by the rigors of a therapy session. Handicapped persons need help in relating to other people and their environment before insight therapy is likely to be of any value. I once encountered an adolescent who confessed in his first interview with me that he was ashamed his mother still helped him bathe. He didn't need help, but was afraid he'd break the glass shampoo bottle. I suggested a plastic substitute and his relief indicated that numerous sessions of insight therapy hadn't helped him solve simple problems of everyday living. Individual guidance or socialization groups normally prove more valuable a learning situation than psychotherapy, although exceptions do exist. A lot depends on the therapist. A few are so exceptional that they can help even the most "difficult" client.

Sex

I know adolescents should be given the facts about sex, but I'm unsure of my handicapped child's ability to handle the information responsibly.

I have been asked many questions about the handicapped and sex. It should be remembered that sexual needs are the same for the handicapped as for other adolescents, and cannot be displaced by substituting other activities. Parents need be concerned the most if their child is uninformed about sex. Don't operate on the assumption that the less he knows, the better off he or she will be—the opposite is true. Answer all questions honestly as they come up and don't save it all for one big tense scene. One of my books that candidly explains sexual functioning and behavior is *Facts About Sex for Today's Youth*, or if your adolescent doesn't like to read, try the comic book *Ten Heavy Facts About Sex*.

The most important messages to convey concern masturbation and sexual behavior. Tell your child that masturbation is normal and no amount of it is harmful provided it is guilt-free and done in private. And among adults sexual behavior is acceptable providing it is voluntary (not compulsive), enjoyable, and nonexploitative of one's partner.

Don't be afraid to take a stand on how you feel, including your feelings about sex outside of marriage, but be sure to add, "When you decide to have sex, here's information on contraception, pregnancy, VD, abortion, and so on." It is a good idea to communicate similar messages about other timely adolescent concerns such as drugs and alcohol. (See Part V, "Resources.")

Thoughts, Fantasies, and Dreams

In remembering what an emotional time adolescence was, I recalled how troubled and guilty I was at times at the nature of some of my thoughts. Now both my wife and I are concerned that our handicapped son will be incapable of understanding what these thoughts mean. ·

The best approach is to simply explain the matter to him. Tell him that he's likely to have suicidal, aggressive, and sexual thoughts and that everyone has them. All thoughts, wishes, dreams, and fantasies are normal. Stress that there is no need to feel guilty, that indeed, he should enjoy and learn from his expanding intellect. Remember, if you are guilty about a thought you will have it over and over again. Make sure he understands that behavior can be wrong but not thoughts.

Repetitions

At times I swear I'll climb the wall if my fourteen-year-old daughter asks me again what time it is, how long it is until such and such happens, or a few other familiar questions. What can I do to end her questioning, or cope with it if it can't be stopped?

Parents are apt to find nothing more aggravating than to be constantly pestered with the same question, which also serves as a constant reminder of the handicap. Even the most patient and well-intentioned people will lose their cool after a while. Yet, there's something that can be done. One of my patients used to ask me the time constantly, until I made a deal with him that I'd tell him the time just three more times, after which I'd count out loud the number of times he'd asked. After a few repetitions he got the point. The objective of breaking such patterns of repetition is to make the youth aware of what he is doing and its impact on people. And such techniques, when substituted for screaming or criticism, keep parents calm as well.

The popular notion that these repetitions are caused by brain damage is not accurate. More often, it is a way of coping with anxiety that should be resolved. In some cases, termination of one repetitive habit may lead to other habits, but often less intolerable ones that at least prove that the repetitions can be stopped.

Siblings' Resentment

Since the care of my handicapped son requires more of my time, my other children resent him. Nothing short of spending equal time with them has soothed their feelings. Can I somehow make them understand?

There is, naturally, concern among siblings that all receive "equal" amounts of parental love and affection, as with equal allowances, birthday and Christmas gifts, and time spent together. Many families suffer disharmony due to a preoccupation with the handicap of one child, but all family members must be told that such attention is deliberate and necessary, and told why. Emphasize that you love your other children no less and be sure your words and actions genuinely reflect this, but be prepared to accept their anger despite your efforts.

Interest in Learning

It's all very well and good for people to say a child's interest must be stimulated, but I've tried countless things with my teenager (recreation, family activities, special programs, etc.) but

*they haven't worked and she almost totally lacks interest in
anything now.*

Think back. You'd be surprised how people learn things best.
If you were ever at all insecure about your performance in a
certain area, you probably sought times to practice alone or
with perhaps just one other trusted person to alleviate possible
embarrassment.

In a setting of noncompetitive learning with a person they
care for, big "scenes" are avoided and individuals feel freer to
extend themselves and experiment. So bowl in empty alleys to
start, find off-nights at restaurants and movies, and don't make a
big deal of mistakes. Build confidence with compliments and
encouragement and lessen his or her fear of ridicule.

Your teenager may be reluctant or refuse to accompany you
or the family on such outings, and at times you should insist she
come, saying "We usually give you a choice of what you'd
rather do, but we want you to come with us this time and try
it." Often, establishing a schedule of once-a-week outings to
accustom her to getting out will prompt her own desire to do
things. At the beginning, going out with only one parent and no
sibling is best.

If your daughter has no suitable friends to act as guides for
other situations and you as a parent find it difficult, you might
try contacting a local college or university with a special
education program. It is surprising how many college students
volunteer to spend time with a handicapped person on a
one-to-one basis. It is an opportunity to supplement the
theoretical instruction students receive at school with valuable
experience. The duration of the relationship should be agreed
upon in advance to discourage any illusions of permanency.

Employment and Living Away from Home

Our handicapped son is about to complete his formal education at the age of nineteen. As neither he nor my wife and I think it wise for him to live at home indefinitely, a job and independence seem the next step. But what are the chances of a handicapped person getting a decent job, and what preparation or information would be helpful?

For the handicapped adolescent or young adult, finding a job can be one of the most difficult, anxiety-ridden tasks he'll ever face. Overcoming discrimination, inferiority feelings, and hesitancy requires encouragement, activity, and willpower.

Remember that job preparation begins at birth. As the individual matures he should be encouraged to do everything possible for himself. Let the "job" begin at home by doing chores such as sweeping, painting, learning to fix things, and participating in family decisions. And instead of saving employment for a big push into a full-time job, begin with summer jobs and odd jobs as a gentle introduction to the realities of the working world.

Perhaps most important are the individual's personal characteristics that enhance his employability: his motivation, ambition, and self-image. If these have been encouraged by self-reliance and reinforcement from his environment, the chances of a job are much better.

Before looking for a job, indeed, throughout the life of a handicapped person, honest, realistic evaluations of what the person can and cannot do should be ongoing to avoid "impossible dreams" and shattered hopes. During adolescence the handicapped should be allowed to experiment with anything of interest, but if unsuccessful, different activities should be sought. A person who speaks poorly or who can't write well should not try to be a teacher, and someone with poor coordination should avoid manual labor.

For some handicapped, employment is feasible only in sheltered workshops, subsidized employment, or part-time situations. In regular job settings, the buddy system, whereby a friendly experienced employee makes learning the ropes just that much easier, is very effective.

Encourage and prepare your young adult to live away from home in situations ranging from complete independence if possible to supervised living arrangements as are now becoming available in halfway houses. There is no reason why a person who has a handicap should be required to live at home unless extraordinary circumstances make no other choice possible. Many handicapped adults become quite resourceful when they must feed, clothe, and care for themselves, as opposed to the feelings of helplessness accompanying total dependence where everything is done for them.

The choice of a job requires determination, imagination, good counseling, and some luck. Keep in mind that it is unwise to place all your hopes on one thing. For instance, vocational placement agencies are often helpful and should be used, but are hardly perfect. "Sure things" may fall through, employers and employees may discriminate, and you may become depressed, but keep at it.

Marriage

How can you tell if a handicapped person is prepared or ever will be prepared to get married? My daughter is set on marriage someday, but I'd hate to see her building false hopes if it really wouldn't be possible.

The most important determining factors in whether or not a

person with a handicap should get married are (1) if one is emotionally mature and sure of one's feelings; (2) one appears reasonably capable of handling the responsibilities associated with marriage. Marriage is a desirable lifestyle for many people who have handicaps.

People get married for love, trust, security, sex, old age, money, and many other reasons. One need only be sure that one's motives for getting married are sound, as determined by how one has handled many other responsibilities in one's life. In this respect, preparation for marriage begins early in life. Extended "engagements" are a perfectly acceptable way to test the relationship to see how things might work out. Parents should not be overprotective or pessimistic about the chances for success. However, we all need to be aware of the fact that marriage is no cure-all or bed of roses even for the nonhandicapped; one in three marriages now ends in divorce or separation.

What about children?

People often express concern that the child of one or two handicapped persons will inherit the handicap. It is advisable for the couple to seek genetic counseling to confirm or allay their fears, and the outcome should be a factor in whatever decision is reached.

In many respects, people have a right to get married, but people have no right to bring a child into the world they can't adequately care for. Marriages of handicapped couples often succeed where there are no children, and in some cases where only one or two children are born. Larger families generally tend to inflict additional responsibilities and burdens on the already handicapped individual. Check with your doctor or local Planned Parenthood Association for further information.

Socialization Groups and Organizations

I've heard of parents and their children getting together in groups with others in similar situations, but any attempts to establish a program in my area have met with lack of information or disinterest. What is the best procedure and what are the pitfalls?

Schools and professional counselors should know best how to connect you with other parents, and together you can organize into socialization groups. Parents and their children should meet separately for mutual benefit.

In such groups, the handicapped, whose adjustment and interaction with "normal" peers has been seriously limited or absent, are given the opportunity to relate meaningfully to other people. They can, without embarrassment or guilt, admit personal deficiencies such as not knowing how to order or tip in a restaurant, how to use a telephone book, date, develop hobbies. As such skills and knowledge are mastered, with the help of the group leaders, a feeling of self-confidence and worth enables the handicapped to expand activities and independence outside as well as inside the group. In addition, purely recreational and fun activities should be part of this experience.

In separate meetings the parents could exchange ideas, feelings, and experiences that could be mutually helpful.

Some established organizations, especially those for the blind, deaf, and severely physically handicapped, sometimes function as vested-interest groups designed to keep in power elite bureaucratic do-gooders. Parents should exert their influence and assume control of these groups.

Remember, organizations serve two important functions: (1) to educate the handicapped about their legal and social rights and insure they are obtained; (2) to create social situations and opportunities designed to enhance their relationships with people and their own self-image. Most groups work in the better interests of the handicapped, but a good way to determine this is their willingness to work with other groups, the effectiveness of coalitions formed, the degree of control parents themselves exercise, and most important, the responses of the handicapped.

Interaction with Handicapped versus "Normal"

I've been told I shouldn't permit my adolescent to be only with other handicapped youngsters. Don't segregated groups encourage this?

Let's get one thing straight. Any handicapped person who can learn and grow by interacting with others should do so. Here we must be concerned with those handicapped individuals who have not been integrated in regular programs.

Let the social experiences with handicapped peers be a rehearsal for other relationships. Having already acquired a minimum of social skills with his own peers, the youth will function more adequately in the more competitive society of nonhandicapped teenagers. If we concentrate on these abilities and positive growth aspects instead of worrying that the handicapped may associate only with other handicapped people, our efforts will pay off.

We have to stop thinking in terms of all-or-none projects and learn to appreciate the partial, nearly imperceptible growth occurring daily that makes entrance into the nonhandicapped world possible.

Pets

Our handicapped daughter has insisted for some time that we get her a dog, and we are naturally concerned for our child's and the dog's welfare. Any thoughts?

A dog cannot enter any household unless it will be readily accepted by all members of the family and no physical aversions such as allergies exist. In the case of tropical fish, hamsters, and the like, no problems are likely to arise. With a larger, more active animal like a cat or dog, however, problems sometimes appear.

Every parent considering a pet must realize that there is a pretty good chance the youth will lose interest and you'll be stuck with the care of the pet yourself. Feeding, grooming, walking, and playing with the animal must occur regularly. As too often is the case, everyone loves the pet to distraction, but reluctantly does the necessary work and becomes ingenious at inventing excuses for not doing so.

Youth are easily excited by the prospect of a pet, which provides opportunities to express love and affection. Getting a dog, for instance, should not be a bribe or reward; the main focus should be care and responsibility for the animal. A pet can be a lovable companion for any child, provided the whole family agrees to accept it, and responsibility for it.

Getting Away

After hearing of a summer camp designed especially for the needs of handicapped teenagers, we suggested to our son that it might be fun for him. He accused us of trying to get rid of him and adamantly refused to go. We were reluctant to force the issue, and as a result he never went. What's a good way to handle this?

I've found that often, regardless of initial apprehension and concern, teenagers who have handicaps wind up enjoying themselves at these places. A few weeks away from home with congenial relatives can be a valuable experience in a new environment as well.

Parents are understandably dismayed by their adolescents' accusations, but it is best if their own guilt and fear of their teenagers' reactions doesn't change their minds if they feel it is best for their child to get away. It is appropriate to force the issue if at all possible, knowing that the experience will probably be appreciated by the adolescent once his original anxieties disappear.

13

Bill of Rights for Parents

Parents are acutely aware of their responsibilities to provide educational, medical, emotional, and professional help for their offspring, but are seldom aware of the rights they also have as parents of a child who has a handicap and as just plain people.

Freedom To:

Love and enjoy your child.

Feel that you have done the best you can.

Be depressed or have hostile thoughts once in a while without feeling guilty.

Be guilty occasionally but only if it organizes you.

Not always feel you have to be patient.

Enjoy life as intensely as possible, even though you have a child who has a handicap.

Have interesting causes to support and to be busier than

the average person, to a point where people say "How does he or she do it?" (If you want something done, ask a busy person.)

Let your handicapped child have his or her own private life.

Enjoy being alone at times.

Get away for at least a two-week vacation every year without the children.

Have dates, anniversaries, celebrations, weekends away, time together designed to enhance your marriage or "singlehood"—in other words, freedom for escapist moments.

Have a sense of humor without feeling guilty.

Acknowledge you are spending lots of time with your child without having it mean you love the rest of the family less.

Not devote your entire life to the "cause," but freedom to devote as much as you want or to get away for a while.

Say at times you don't want to talk about your problems.

Let people know at other times about the progress and achievements with a genuine sense of pride.

Lie every once in a while, to say everything is fine, not feeling compelled to tell the truth to everyone who asks, "How are you?"

Tell teachers and other professionals how you really feel about the job they are doing and to demand they respect your opinions.

Tell your child you don't like certain things he or she does, even though he or she has a handicap.

Not praise your child gratuitously even though you've been told to offer a lot of praise.

Spend a little extra money on yourself whether or not you can afford it.

Have your hobbies and interests without interference whether Mah-Jongg, Mahler, or macrame.

Warning: Parents who do not enjoy almost all these freedoms are in trouble. Persons who have handicaps will feel guilty when they sense that their parents have sacrificed themselves for them. Martyred parents are seldom appreciated by anybody, least of all their handicapped child. These freedoms must be embarked upon especially by parents whose child has been dependent, clinging, demanding, and difficult.

14

For Brothers and Sisters

It seems only natural to include here a message for brothers and sisters of people who have handicaps. Each person in any family influences the environment and relationships among its members. With this in mind, we'd like to help put you in closer touch with your siblings and parents, and vice versa.

There are many different family situations and ways of dealing with the problems involved. In some families there is a general atmosphere of good spirit and acceptance of each other. You may be able to understand the feelings and behavior of your brother or sister and balance them with your own needs. This is most important: If each family member can maintain a balance of priorities and keep things in perspective with a good sense of humor, fewer problems develop.

It is rarely if ever helpful to sacrifice one's own interests and activities to "help" your sibling although some extra help is usually welcome. Giving up friends or career development creates a handicap for you as well. Don't convince yourself that your sibling will love you more if you pay more attention to him or her—the quality, not quantity, counts the most. On the other hand, a good number of siblings have gone into the special education field and have been helpful and established a career, motivated by concern for a brother or sister. If your sibling senses that he or she is burdening you and depriving you of time and attention to yourself, he or she will probably feel guilty and unhappy as the result. Unfortunately, they may sometimes express this by being even more demanding of you.

If you feel comfortable about it, discuss your feelings and anxieties with your parents, who may be able to offer some realistic suggestions. Some families experience great difficulty in adjusting to one person's handicap. It can be hard to cope with a sibling who is isolated, inactive, clinging, or dependent. You may resent the extra attention he or she receives and time you may be forced to spend together. Perhaps you feel deprived of the companionship brothers and sisters usually share. Since a disabling condition often places a severe financial strain on parents, you may also feel deprived of material things like vacations and new clothes.

It is also normal to have negative thoughts about your handicapped brother or sister: wishing they were dead; would go away; were never born; and so on. In fact, it is common for the person with a handicap to have similar thoughts about other family members when they aren't getting along. People often become guilty about these bad feelings, but as we've suggested in Chapter 9 and Chapter 1, only behavior is wrong. It is important to realize that if you feel guilty about a thought, you probably won't be able to help having that same thought over and over again. If you can accept these feelings as just one of many different ones, you won't be so overwhelmed by them.

An ambivalent response to a handicapped sibling is inevitable. Our feelings go through periods of differing moods and changes, loves and hates, for the same person. You can't expect to love a sibling, handicapped or not, all of the time. Yet, even if you sincerely love more than dislike your brother or sister, he or she may be so insecure as to believe you dislike him or her most of the time. If you suspect this is true, tell your sibling directly how you really feel, and explain that sometimes you just can't avoid becoming angry. Understanding that there is a range of emotions in everyone frees us to accept even angry feelings without becoming preoccupied with them.

But don't respond by feeling guilty and never expressing resentment to a handicapped brother or sister or anyone else. Honest feelings of anger should be expressed and talked over to let your sibling know what kind of impression he or she makes on you and on other people.

It is important to understand that people with serious problems may tend to complain a lot, feel sorry for themselves, and be very passive (mope around, watch TV, have no interests). To other people this is usually boring and hard to handle, and it may result in the person having no friends.

Have you ever felt you were clumsy, unintelligent, incompetent, or unattractive, or felt you weren't worth much? Feeling inadequate and worthless is one of the biggest problems many people with handicaps must deal with. People's self-images suffer the most when they compare themselves with people they consider to be more attractive, luckier, or more intelligent. Everyone can help by not boasting, and by not belittling or teasing a person with a handicap. In addition, don't be afraid to tell your sister or brother when you are proud of her or him and that she or he is doing a good job.

It is best if your interaction and time spent together is voluntary. Sometimes you may be forced to spend time together against your will and best judgment. At these times, it is good to make the best of it and not to generate more anger. If possible, make your own arrangements for activities together and set aside specific times during the day for each other. Sometimes giving it a little structure of preplanned time eliminates the need for parental interference. And if not done out of anger (not necessarily love—but perhaps a sense of responsibility or commitment) your concern may be appreciated. Once you have developed a good relationship and some intimacy, you will be in a better position to communicate and give advice, to explain feelings.

Encourage your siblings to be active and to develop hobbies and interests of their own. A big problem people with handicaps have is being bored, watching too much television, rarely going out. If you can share your time and belongings and include your sister or brother occasionally in your fun, the result could be a more stimulated person. By spending a little extra time and energy to get him or her started, you can avoid problems later on and even save time you need for yourself.

This brings up the problem of how to orient your friends to the situation. The worst thing is to assume they'll be unsympathetic and cruel and to avoid inviting them to your home to prevent being embarrassed. Also, there's no use pretending that nothing is wrong and hoping your friends will figure out for themselves how to relate to your sibling.

Explain the nature of the handicap without making excuses or asking for pity. Try to convey that your brother's or sister's feelings and desires are like anybody else's. This of course implies that he or she needs friendship and the feeling of being part of a group, and that he or she is hurt when people make fun of him or her.

Regardless of your efforts and concern, some people, strangers included, invariably make nasty jokes and comments. You might respond, according to the situation, with a sense of humor, by asking them not to be unkind, or by ignoring them. If you strike back, you are allowing yourself to be provoked, which is what the other person intended to do. Don't play the game.

Sometimes people with handicaps require special schooling in some form or another. The disability often makes it more difficult for them to read, concentrate, write, speak, turn the pages—you know your own situation. You or your friends might misinterpret this and think it makes them "stupid," but it simply means that they must learn differently from other people, not that they can't learn.

We are sensitive to the fact that we have focused mainly on conflicts and problems in this section because their resolution and alleviation is the main purpose of this book. We are aware of the fact that in many homes the person with a handicap inspires confidence, interest, and feelings of joy and well-being. He or she is often a source of great stimulation for siblings and parents to achieve and develop their own selves as much as possible. There are even families where the people with handicaps are so well integrated and accepted that they cause virtually no problems.

When you get down to it, there's no one like a family member to be able to count on. If you don't get along very well with your brothers or sisters now, people might say, "You'll grow out of it someday," which may or not be true in your case. If you don't get along, try to understand some of the things this book stands for. Explore the possibility of working in the direction of enjoying each other's company and helping each other out. A brother or sister with a handicap can be just as much fun as anyone else—if he or she can't run or wrestle around or whatever, he or she certainly can do other things and share them with you.

In closing we offer our hope that you'll be one of those people who are able to understand and cooperate while maintaining a balance between yourself and your sibling. You may be interested in reading other portions of this book, especially those written for people with handicaps, and for parents. If you can get together with the rest of the family, you'll have overcome the main handicap a handicap creates.

15

The Parent of an Adolescent Who Has a Handicap Speaks to Us All

by Betty Lou Kratoville

The quality of independence may be the greatest gift a parent can bestow upon a child. Yet it is often one of the most difficult, involving, as it does, the emotional involvement of "letting go." Parents must be willing and able to let go not only physically ("Yes, you can go on a weekend camping trip with the fellows") but intellectually ("Whether or not you continue to go to church is up to you"). How much easier said than done! This is especially true in today's world with all of its dangers, real and implied. And when the child has a handicap, the wish to shelter and protect him or her is multiplied many times over. It is so much easier to keep him or her safe, to keep him or her happy, if carefully kept under the family's wing. Nothing can happen to him or her. *We* won't let it!

Therein lies the problem. Nothing will happen—none of the

good things, none of the unfortunate things, none of the learning experiences that accompany risk, none of the joy that comes from independent action, none of the satisfaction that comes from making one's own decisions. The child—and later the teenager—is, with the best of intentions, insulated from all experiential growth, and the basic handicap, whatever it may be, can eventually prove to be the very least of his or her problems.

We all long for pat answers. Take Step One for three weeks, follow with Step Two for two months, and then move into Step Three. Result: independence! How nice if this were so; but, of course, it simply doesn't work this way. One reason is the indisputable fact that all children are different. Some reach out for independence on the very first day they find themselves up and walking—it's out the door, through the yard, and into the treacherous streets. Other youngsters seem naturally fearful, afraid to stray very far from their mothers' presence. In this respect, the handicapped do not differ from the so-called normal youngster but for some reason their natural proclivity toward recklessness or timidity provokes more response—just as everything else that they do or do not do, can or cannot do, is maximized by the adults in their lives.

Nevertheless, the importance of independence and self-reliance cannot be overemphasized for the handicapped. It is, first of all, critical because of the ego factor, the "I can do" ingredient. Handicapped youngsters need to feel involvement with their own destinies, need to feel capable of making their own decisions, need to profit from their own mistakes. Only in this way can they possibly come to regard themselves as well-rounded, worthwhile, dependable human beings. Second, from the purely practical standpoint, the ability to take independent action is vitally important. Probability, in its purest sense, indicates that the parent will not always be on hand to make decisions or to chart courses or to lead the way, and so it becomes a matter of survival. The handicapped person must become independent unless he or she is to be institutionalized or turned over to relatives. Someday he or she will quite literally be on his or her own, and this fact should not be decried. Indeed, this is life as it should be lived.

To aid in fostering independence, the young person should first be allowed and encouraged to make minor decisions. Too often we find parents of teenagers still making statements such as the following: "Take your umbrella because it might rain." "Finish your milk." "Did you brush your teeth?" "Oh, you're so pokey, let me do that for you." Parents would be well advised to eliminate all such comments from their conversation. If the adolescent gets uncomfortably soaked, he will remember to take his umbrella next time the weather threatens. Does it really matter whether or not he finishes his milk? Yes, brushing one's teeth is a social nicety and good health principle, but it is up to the adolescent to recognize that fact and deal with his personal grooming accordingly. And, most important of all, no matter how slowly or ineptly a task is being handled, the adolescent must be allowed to finish it himself with no swipes taken at his competence or lack thereof.

The examples given above can be dealt with in a much kinder and in an ego-reinforcing manner—e.g., "It looks like rain. Do *you* think you should take an umbrella?" (The latter is suggested only if the parent simply cannot handle the weather problem and feels impelled to make some sort of comment.) "Shall I put your milk in the refrigerator so that you can finish it later?" leaves the teenager free to make a decision, although half a glass of milk is such a minor matter, it might better be dropped. "I have bought you a new toothbrush and that new brand of toothpaste" is all a parent should be expected to do in regard to personal hygiene. Happily, most teenagers are anxious to appear at their best although, of course, at times what they regard as their "best" does not necessarily coincide with parental views.

In such cases, the teenager's views in the matter of dress, hair styling, and the like should prevail.

Dozens of small opportunities exist daily which the parent can seize to foster independence. Often handicapped adolescents through sheer habit will ask for help in matters they are clearly capable of handling themselves: "May I spend my whole allowance on a birthday present for Janet?" (Suggested response: "You decide—it's your money.") "What shall I get her?" (Suggested response: "Oh, I'm sure you know what she likes much better than I do.") "What shall I wear to the party?" (Suggested response: "What you feel prettiest in.") "What time must I be home?" (Suggested response: "What do you think would be a reasonable time? Ten o'clock? Great!")

Self-reliance in the home can sometimes be nurtured if parents do not mind being a trifle devious. Mother can cultivate an infrequent headache so that family members must fix their own meal. Father's sprained back requires help with bringing in wood for the fireplace or mowing the grass. Everyone likes to feel needed, and this can be an effective way to begin to prove to a youngster that he "can do" as well as anyone else in the family. In such instances, praise should be bestowed liberally and sincerely. "You fixed these hamburgers all by yourself? How marvelous! I didn't know you could do that. Will you fix them when Grandma and Grandpa come for supper Sunday evening?"

Often true independence and efficiency can result from need. One brain-injured fourteen-year-old has turned into a competent cook because his mother works, and he grew tired of cold cereal breakfasts when he slept late in the summer time. Having experienced success with French toast and pancakes, he then turned his hand to luncheon and dinner menus and to baking cakes and cookies.

In summary, parents are advised to hold meddling in minor matters to a minimum and to use their wits in using every conceivable opportunity for moving their handicapped adolescent into independent thought and action.

Employment

As soon as possible, independence on the home front should be extended to community and/or job efforts. "I promised to canvas our block for the United Fund, and now your brother is ill. I'm sure you could do a fine job and probably even beat my record from last year." "Everyone in the neighborhood is getting together to clean out the vacant lot and turn it into a baseball field. Let's help." "Mrs. Brown has broken her ankle. Let's go over and do her washing for her—or would you rather bake her a cake?"

Jobs may pose more of a problem than community and volunteer action but many parents have moved a youngster into the job market through the use of subsidies. "I know you need someone to take care of your lawn. I would like to suggest that you let Larry do it, and I will pay his salary until such time as you feel he is doing the kind of job you are willing to pay for." (Larry is not to know of this arrangement.) "If you will take Carol on as an aide at summer camp, I will underwrite her salary." Usually such strategies need not be prolonged. Once given a chance, the youngster is able to prove her worth, and the subsidy stratagem is set aside.

Fortunate is the family with a business of its own which can use the services of its handicapped young adult. In Texas, one father hired his learning-disabled daughter to work in the family print shop. In a sense it was a desperation move. The girl had graduated from high school with a limited diploma, had no friends, no special interests, no job qualifications. It was understood in advance that she would be given no special treatment or privileges, and the father now freely admits that he initially had very little hope for the success of the experiment. But it worked! His daughter learned her responsibilities with a minimum of error and took them very seriously; she quickly and easily made friends with other employees; and she acquired a number of unexpected skills such as the ability to find her way around the city streets, to handle the mechanics of eating in cafeterias and restaurants, as well as the agreeable business of budgeting and saving her salary. She ultimately decided that she wanted to spend some of her income on ballet lessons, which opened up an entirely new field of interest, and she has since appeared in her first recital. Employing one's own handicapped youngster can be a mutually rewarding experience if parent and child are agreeable and willing to set aside their roles as relatives and to assume the more impersonal roles of employer and employee.

Parents need to research the job market, both from the standpoint of what is suitable for the youngster and to locate those types of employers who are willing to employ the handicapped and to treat them fairly and respectfully. One mother noticed an obviously handicapped young man working as an usher in a neighborhood theater. She immediately contacted the manager and asked that her own handicapped son be considered when a vacancy arose. Within two months her son was given a chance to run the refreshment counter in the theater and has worked weekends and summer vacations ever since.

Parents need to scrutinize junior colleges, community colleges, and trade schools for suitable job training for their young adult. It is well to examine carefully the credentials of all schools, especially those that promise job placement, making sure that they do intend to fulfill their promises. Today there are many, many trades and professions which can be filled by the handicapped. Unless the adolescent's physical or mental limitations are extremely severe, there should be a job for him if parents are willing to research the subject. In the case of severe limitations, it is hoped that the parent will be very clever and tireless in order to structure creative, meaningful jobs and responsibilities on the home front and, if possible, in the neighborhood.

Socialization

Surely parents who have been willing to make every effort to see that their child received an adequate education should be equally willing to put forth similar effort into insuring that an adequate social life is also provided. How best to do it? There are many avenues to pursue although not all are suitable for every family or every situation.

An easy and pleasant ruse is to make the home an inviting place where people like to gather. The age of the guest really doesn't matter that much. Live, warm bodies are the important prerequisite because the more experience a handicapped youngster has with many individuals, younger or older, the more it will help him to feel at ease with people of all ages, including his own. One family went deeply into debt and put in the only swimming pool in the neighborhood. Friends and relatives and neighborhood children flocked to it, often bringing their own refreshments but always bringing their own uniqueness. Not only did the handicapped adolescent in that family have a built-in social life, he also became an excellent swimmer, eventually joining a community swimming team and bringing home a fine collection of ribbons.

Obviously the attraction need not always be as elaborate as a pool. It can be a Ping-Pong or pool table or a badminton court or a croquet court or simply a pleasant room well stocked with games and records and easy accessibility to the refrigerator. It can be a spur-of-the-moment "everybody come to our house.

We're going to make popcorn balls" or "Come on over and help us paint the fence, and then I'll fix a barbecue for everyone." Any of these approaches can constitute the beginning of social growth for the handicapped youngster; no matter if it is calculated, as long as it works. Eventually, the "attraction" will become the developed personality of the youngster himself.

Some families, especially if both the mother and father work or if it is a one-parent family, have solved part of the problem of a social life for the lonely teenager by hiring a high school or college student to serve as a companion. In this way there is no end to the activities that can be planned: camping trips, movies, concerts, picnics, shopping, expeditions to the local museum, art gallery, or zoo. Such a companion, of course, must be carefully selected in regard to reliability and empathy. On many campuses, the services are volunteered by social workers or other students.

Families should also stay alert to various community social groups which have demonstrated their willingness to work with the handicapped: Boy Scouts, Girl Scouts, square dance groups, athletic groups, hobby clubs, and young people's church groups. All such organizations must be carefully researched to be sure that their members are of suitable caliber to welcome a handicapped youngster and to recognize his or her intrinsic worth. One epileptic girl, aged nineteen, was quite literally dying of loneliness. She had been forced through an unrelated illness to leave college for the semester and had finally reached such a point of boredom and despair that she took to her bed. A family friend invited her to attend guest night at a local ballroom-dancing studio. The evening was such a success that the girl enrolled in a series of lessons, worked diligently with the staff, who were quite aware of her handicap and who over-looked an occasional seizure, and she eventually danced com-petitively with great success and joy.

Occasionally two handicapped youngsters will hit it off and

become fast friends. Strangely, some parents find this hard to accept. "But he is much worse than our child, who should be with more normal people" is sometimes the attitude. Nonsense! If one handicapped teenager is perceptive enough to recognize something of value in another handicapped person, it should be a matter of pride and something rather lovely to watch.

To summarize briefly, parents are urged to cease wringing their hands and bemoaning their child's loneliness, replacing this study in futility with serious thought and sustained action in order to solve this most critical need of the handicapped. Frequently results will be achieved that were never sought or expected and that will prompt enormous family pride and relief and triumph.

Communication

Communication unquestionably holds a position of high priority on the long list of parental duties and responsibilities involved in the rearing of a handicapped individual. The need for opening up lines of communication begins early, often when the family may still be reeling under the impact of diagnosis. ("What do we tell our friends or the grandparents or the other children in the family?") The need continues through the years as the family moves from one place to another, as new neighbors and friends are woven into the family fabric, as new situations and encounters occur. This is particularly true when the handicap is a hidden or subtle one such as brain injury, learning disabilities, epilepsy, or a moderate hearing deficit.

The concern about what to tell to whom and how much has been compounded in recent years when parents have often had to assume an instructional role with professionals. If the diagnosis has been a psychological or educational one, it has sometimes been necessary for parents to acquaint and enlighten the family doctor on the nature of the handicap, especially if his help is needed with medication or diet. If the diagnosis has been a medical one, parents have had to find ways to reach teachers who have had no special training. How best to approach a scout leader, a Sunday school teacher, or even salespeople who are obviously disenchanted with a clumsy adolescent who is prone to bump into displays of merchandise or to talk in a loud or embarrassing manner?

Each day, all of these people cut a wide swath through the lives of a handicapped person and his family. Their impact can be brutalizing if not downright fatal—or, conversely, it can contribute to the rehabilitative processes. These individuals must be dealt with—effectively and courageously—to the point where simple communication becomes almost an exercise in the art of public relations.

It is difficult to generalize or to lay down specific procedures because of the enormous variations in people and in situations. However, one rule of thumb seems to have merit in most (not all) situations: Communication in the form of explanation and education *is* required if the family is to have an ongoing relationship with an individual—i.e., neighbor, friend, doctor, relative, or teacher. Communication in the form of explanation and education is *not* required if a chance or one-time encounter is involved.

Once a decision has been made that some form of communication is indicated, how can one best do it? It is certain the handicapped individual should never be present during such an exchange. An optimum setting should be sought, a time that is both convenient and relaxed for all involved. The key word is explanation, not apology. This is the way it is, this is the way it will be, this is what we are doing about it. This is how we need your understanding. This is how we need your help. Since the printed word is apt to command respect, reading material may be an excellent approach but it should be simple, straightforward, nontechnical, and, if possible, brief. It is safe to say that informative material can now be found on every handicapping condition. Sources include the public library and organizations which have been formed to deal with specific handicaps such as the Alexander Graham Bell Association for the Deaf, the American Schizophrenia Foundation, the Epilepsy Foundation of America, the National Association for Retarded Children, the National Easter Seal Society for Crippled Children and Adults, the United Cerebral Palsy Association, the Association for Children with Learning Disabilities. (The parent uses such sources not only for purposes of communicating with others but also to keep himself informed about new developments, methods, procedures, legislation, and so on.)

Parents of the handicapped will learn as time passes how to "read" the people with whom they must communicate about their child. It becomes almost an intuitive thing. One learns to sense if a lengthy description is required or if a more perfunctory one will do the job. If the ear of the listener seems less than sympathetic, it may be better to postpone the conversation, or on some sad occasions the parent may simply have to give up. The whole world is not yet ready to listen or to care about the handicapped, and parents must be grateful for those loyal, compassionate people who do attend, take heed, and help.

Parents must take care to emphasize that they are not seeking pity for themselves or their youngster. Pity is not constructive and can even prolong feelings of inertia, guilt, and frustration. The recommended point of view is one that is upbeat, matter-of-fact, and optimistic. One can imply, in effect, "Our family is determined to meet this challenge, and we will never stop looking for answers."

Once a line of communication has been established with friends, neighbors, and relatives, there is no need to belabor the subject. If further questions are forthcoming, they should be dealt with in an honest and forthright fashion. Remember that a handicapping condition, like other family concerns, is more interesting and vital to the involved family than to anyone else and should not be dwelt on to the point of saturation and boredom.

Siblings in the family of a handicapped youth should be privy to as much information as they can comprehend. The older children can be given the facts clinically and objectively. Occasionally, if their parents are distraught and overwhelmed by the handicapping condition, they may as well know it. But the burden is not theirs, and if they now and then seem callous or unfeeling, they should not be penalized, but they must be allowed their own pursuits, interests, and joys. Children are very perceptive, and the parent must be prepared for questions which are not always easy to answer, feeling free to say, "I don't know the answer to that question" if, indeed, he does not and, perhaps, to add, "I'll try to find out."

It would seem better for all concerned if younger children in the family were not involved in long, easily misinterpreted explanations until they are old enough to sense and inquire about the problem. Occasions may conceivably arise when the handicapped sibling's behavior or lack of response will cause them grief or pain. At such times, parents should rise to the occasion and deal with their feelings. It should also be recognized that children have a way of accepting bizarre situations which adults do not have, that they often devise their own methods for coping and are, perhaps, stronger and wiser for the experience. If they can rely on their parents for honest information, frank answers, and an equitable relationship among all the members of the family, they will respond in kind.

This is what communication with others is all about—the need to cultivate the ability to open doors, minds, and hearts to the plight and the problems of the handicapped and his family. It will be helpful to take the long view which holds the conviction that light focused on specific problems of specific children will add to the general knowledge and will serve all children well. Such an attitude on the part of parents is bound to increase their dedication, to stiffen their determination, and, quite simply, to ennoble the cause.

Communicating with the Handicapped

Much has been written in recent years about whether or not a person with a terminal illness should be told the truth about his condition. The authorities occasionally come close to agreement with the premise that it depends on the individual's ability to handle news of such tragic import. Advocates of the "give it to them straight" theory call this a "cop-out" as, in some cases, it may be. The same theory would seem to have validity in dealing with the handicapped, who need to know as much about the true extent and degree of their handicapping condition as they can accept without extinguishing the spark of life that propels us all. Most parents, as the years go by, learn how much or how little their children can bear.

There seems to be little point in volunteering information which the handicapped adolescent has not demanded. In such cases, he has probably drawn his own conclusions and is trying to live with them. In the case of questions, the parent would be well advised to answer them as truthfully as possible, even if the answer must sometimes be "I don't know." More often than not, this is truly the case in a day when science, medicine, and education progress at such breathtaking speed. Many handicapping conditions regarded as hopeless a decade ago have much hope for improvement today. In such an age, it is happily almost impossible to put a ceiling on the potential of any individual. It is true—we do *not* know.

In those cases where we do not have a firm answer but are

queried by the handicapped youngster, it seems ethical whenever possible to tell the truth but to use one's wits and one's
humanity when doing so. Even the tortured cry "Why was I
born?" can be dealt with gently—i.e., "Because you have much
to give, and the world has much to give to you." A handicapped
adolescent may deny this in moments of anguish but with the
help of parents and others who love him and who recognize his
need for reassurance, he will one day come to believe life does
hold promise and meaning. Yet he must constantly be given new
opportunities to grow, to learn, to explore, to communicate, to
reach out, to try, perhaps to fail, but to try again.

If parents always remember that handicapped youngsters are
more like normal youngsters than unlike them, it will be easier
to hold to a healthy perspective, to communicate in natural
terms, to realize that no child can be protected from all pain or
should be. The handicapped do deserve and require extra
attention, special planning, extraordinary support, and encouragement. In return, however, the parent can expect unparal-
leled satisfaction and pride in the acknowledgment of demands
well met and a job well done. The parent, or the friend, or the
teacher, of a handicapped youngster who has responded to a cry
for help with a full measure of concern and intelligence and
love serves himself, his charge, and all of humanity well.

16

Survival in the Rehab Jungle

by Charles Weening

Eleven years in a State Rehabilitation Agency taught me that people found out about these services in some strange ways. Usually, they were "sent" to me with little or no idea of the services available. I have a standing bet, which no one has taken, that if you stopped ten people on the street and asked, "What is Vocational Rehabilitation?" only one or two would have some vague idea of what was involved.

This is really amazing since the program has been established since 1920. Perhaps the tug of war about the Vocational Rehabilitation Act of 1973 helped to make the program more well known. All political issues aside, you, as a parent of a handicapped child, should be aware of your rights under this program.

The original legislation was designed to help physically

handicapped veterans after World War I. A series of changes made the services available to all the handicapped.

Under this law, each state and territory has a Vocational Rehabilitation Agency. It is supported by 80 percent federal funds and 20 percent state or local funds. These state agencies are charged with providing services to help handicapped people of *working age* enter, or reenter, employment. That means their job is vocational in nature and the services are provided only to those people who *probably* can enter employment.

Meeting the eligibility requirement (see Glossary in Chapter 17) is like walking between two electric fences—if you touch either one you're in trouble. One fence is disability. That is, you must establish that a disability exists which creates limitations. The limitations must be a handicap to employment.

The other fence is practicability. This means that there is some expectation that the disabled person can engage in gainful employment. Saying this another way, he is not so disabled that he can't work.

These are the federally established eligibility requirements for the vocational rehabilitation program:

1. Disability
2. Limitations
3. Employment handicap
4. Employability

A rehab counselor must actually list these things in a case record, with medical and other reports to prove eligibility, before any services can be given.

Once these facts are in the record, the person is eligible to receive all of the services the agency provides. You say there has to be a catch, and there is. The person is entitled only to those services absolutely *necessary* to achieve a *specific vocational goal* (carpenter, nurse, etc.).

What kinds of service? Medical service extends from things as simple as a brace to as complicated as open-heart surgery. It also includes psychotherapy.

Training services from a couple of weeks of brush-up at a secretarial school to a full college education are offered.

Counseling, guidance, and help with job placement are provided as well.

You are probably saying to yourself, "What a wonderful program!" You're right! Let's make sure that you know how to establish eligibility for these services.

LESSON 1

Stay with the familiar. If there are two or three names for the same thing, use the most-easy-to-understand disability name. Make sure it gets across the idea of disability.

The first thing you must remember is to deal with the bureaucratic mind. If you tell a rehab counselor that your child has acromegaly or some other ten-dollar word, you will not receive services. He won't know what it means and is too professional to look it up.

LESSON 2

It's important that you can show limitations imposed by the disability in order to establish the employment handicap.

If the application says, "How does the disability limit function" do *not* write "none." If you do, you will probably get a form politely telling you to get lost.

LESSON 3

This is very important! Whether or not a given disability is or is not a handicap to employment is a matter of opinion. It depends on the limitations and the knowledge and experience of the person making the decision. The tip which was cut off my pinky is not a handicap in most vocations. If I were a violinist when the accident happened, it would have required rehab services to help me prepare for a job in another field. You can hand the same case folder to two rehab administrators and have one say yes and the other no. When it comes to employment

handicap, pray that your rehab counselor doesn't have a
hangover.

LESSON 4

*You should be prepared to show how the disability and
limitations would keep your child from entering those vocations
in keeping with his aptitudes, interests, and needs.*

That last part is one of the pet catch phrases in rehab,
especially when they are trying to close a case as a successful
rehab. You should practice using the phrase. If you don't think
that the services provided are in keeping with your child's
aptitudes, interests, and needs, be prepared to say so—loudly.

What this really means is, are the vocational (job) objectives
and services being offered appropriate?

LESSON 5

*Do not let things go too long in choosing a vocational
objective.* Through your school and other sources begin to
explore possible vocations with your child. (Many colleges and
universities have low-cost testing programs.)

LESSON 6

Do not let anyone stereotype your child.

Just because a child is blind does not mean that he should
spend his life in a sheltered workshop, and not all people in
wheelchairs should sell light bulbs over the telephone.

LESSON 7

*Do not agree to a vocational objective until all parties
concerned are in agreement.*

Most rehab agencies have a rule against "upgrading": They
believe that they were established to help the needy, not the
greedy. Let me give an example. Suppose rehab decided to send
your child to a four-year college for a degree in chemistry.
Halfway through he decides that he would prefer to become a
doctor. This change in vocational objectives would mean a great
deal more time and expense. It would be difficult to get the
rehab people to go along with the change.

LESSON 8

Provide as much diagnostic material as you can in the beginning. Make sure you sign releases for things like hospital records. Call your counselor frequently to make sure he is still awake.

The diagnostic phase of the rehab program often takes a long time. There are two reasons: Information has to be gathered from a number of sources like schools and hospitals; also, they will not take Step 3 until they have taken Step 2. Example: A hard-of-hearing child would not be sent to a hearing specialist until a general medical report was received. This phase should last no longer than ninety days.

LESSON 9

If you have been given two opinions on the same subject, demand to see the "Administrative Manual" or "Rules and Regs."

In most states, the rules and regulations which govern a public agency are a public document—and do not take force until they have been "published" or given public hearing.

This will also help you to avoid being put in a bind by a change in counselors.

LESSON 10

The more knowledge you and other parents have about the rehab program the better services you will receive.

If you are knowledgeable about rehab services, you *will* get better service. However, if you come on too strong, you tend to get people irritated. *Do not* irritate an experienced bureaucrat. You will lose more than you gain and use up energy that could be used elsewhere.

Remember that the rehab program was created to help the disabled, not to create bureaucratic jobs. People who have been rehabilitated pay back five dollars for every dollar invested in them in federal taxes alone. So it's no welfare program.

Ask for a speaker and specifically request that he bring along written materials.

When the rehab budget is bottled up in committee, the parents' groups are the ones who have to help restore cuts and get it passed. A strong parent group gets things done—join one. If there are none, start one.

Rehab eligibility policies and services are, in large part, determined by federal legislation. However, vocational rehabilitation is highly individualized. Each client is evaluated in terms of his personal needs and a program of service is designed accordingly. It does not operate like MDTA or other manpower agencies. Whatever services an individual client needs are purchased from whatever sources are available.

In all cases the rehab agency pays for diagnostic services and provides free counseling, job placement, and follow-up. The R.A. will pay all or part of the cost of medical restoration and training, depending on the client's financial situation. The financial needs test is usually not structured like that of welfare, in that a person does not need to be at the poverty level to receive help.

The next section is a sample case I made up to show how the rehab program works. Of course, not every person would need all the services described.

An Example of Vocational Rehabilitation

An eighteen-year-old named John is about to be graduated from high school and is referred to rehab because he had a driving accident that paralyzed him from the waist down (paraplegia). He submits a simple application form to the R.A. and is assigned a rehabilitation counselor from the office near his home. In an interview the counselor obtains basic information about John's medical, educational, social, and employment history. The counselor also purchases a general medical exam from John's family doctor, requests further information from the doctor who attended him after his accident, and calls John's school about his grades and test scores.

Based on the information he gathers during this diagnostic period, which may include other special exams suggested by John's doctor and last anywhere from two weeks to several months, the counselor determines John's eligibility for services and learns about his vocational potential.

John is found eligible because he has a disability, and because orthopedic treatment and further education should help him overcome his disability and become employable. Since John's family has only enough income to cover living expenses and the tuition of his elder brother who is already in college, it is decided that rehab will pay the cost of restoration and training.

17

A Glossary of Rehabilitation Terms

by Charles Weening

You will notice that this glossary is not in alphabetical order. Each definition leads to the next idea and, if you read this a couple of times, you will have the necessary ammunition to bag some rehab service.

I. Legal Terms
These are definitions from Federal Register, Volume 31, No. 9, HR15827 3-7-68.

ELIGIBILITY

When used in relation to an individual's qualifications for vocational rehabilitation services, refers to a certification that (1) the handicapped individual has a physical or mental disability which constitutes a substantial handicap to employment and (2) vocational rehabilitation services may reasonably be expected to render him fit to engage in a gainful occupation.

GAINFUL OCCUPATION — Includes employment in the competitive labor market; practice of a profession; self-employment; homemaking; farm or family work (including work for which payment is in kind rather than in cash); sheltered employment; and home industries or other gainful homebound work.

HANDICAPPED INDIVIDUAL — Means any individual who has a physical or mental disability which constitutes a substantial handicap to employment, but which is of such a nature that vocational rehabilitation services may reasonably be expected to render him fit to engage in a gainful occupation, including a gainful occupation which is more consistent with his capacities and abilities.

MAINTENANCE — Means payments to cover the handicapped individual's basic living expenses, such as food, shelter, clothing, health maintenance, and other subsistence expenses essential to determination of the individual's rehabilitation potential or to achievement of his vocational rehabilitation objective.

PHYSICAL OR MENTAL DISABILITY — Means a physical or mental condition which materially limits, contributes to limiting, or, if not corrected, will probably result in limiting an individual's activities or functioning. It includes behavioral disorders characterized by deviant social behavior or impaired ability to carry out normal relationships with family and community which may result from vocational, educational, cultural, social, environmental, or other factors.

PHYSICAL RESTORATION SERVICES — Means those medical and medically related services which are necessary to correct or substantially modify within a reasonable period of time a physical or mental condition which is stable or slowly progressive, and includes: (1) mental or medical specialists; (2) psychiatric treatment; (3) dentistry; (4) nursing services; (5) hospitalization (either inpatient or outpatient care); (6) convalescent, nursing or rest home care; (7) drugs and supplies; (8) prosthetic devices essential to obtaining or retaining employment; (9) physical therapy; (10) occupational therapy; (11) medically directed speech or hearing therapy; (12) physical rehabilitation; (13) treatment of medical complications and emergencies either acute or chronic which are associated with or arise out of the provision of physical restoration services, or are inherent in the condition under treatment; and (14) other medical or medically related rehabilitation services. The provision that the condition is stable or slowly progressive does not apply when physical restoration services are provided in order to determine the rehabilitation potential.

PROSTHETIC DEVICE

Means any appliance designed to support or take the place of a part of the body, or to increase the acuity of a sensory organ.

SUBSTANTIAL HANDICAP
TO EMPLOYMENT

Means that a physical or mental disability (in the light of attendant medical, psychological, vocational, educational, cultural, social, or environmental factors) impedes an individual's occupational performance, by preventing his obtaining, retaining, or

REHABILITATION
FACILITY

preparing for a gainful occupation consistent with his capacities and abilities.

The term "rehabilitation facility" means a rehabilitation center, workshop, or other facility operated for the primary purpose of assisting handicapped individuals and providing evaluation and work adjustment services for disadvantaged individuals, and which provides singly or in combination one or more of the following services for handicapped individuals: (1) Comprehensive rehabilitation services which shall include, under one management, medical, psychological, social, and vocational services, (2) testing, fitting, or training, in the use of prosthetic devices, (3) prevocational conditioning or recreational therapy, (4) physical and occupational therapy, (5) speech and hearing pathology, (6) psychological and social services, (7) evaluation, (8) personal and work adjustment, (9) vocational training in combination with other services, (10) evaluation or control of special disabilities, and (11) extended employment for the severely handicapped who cannot be readily absorbed in the competitive labor market; but all medical and related services must be prescribed by, or under the formal supervision of, persons licensed to practice medicine or surgery in the state.

II. Terms Used in the Rehabilitation Process and in Ordinary Conversation

These are my own definitions.

VOCATIONAL TRAINING   Used in its broad sense, includes institutional training from brush-up at a
business college to a full four-year
college program, trade schools, and
on-the-job training. It is not provided
to get around a disability but to train
the individual to reach his maximum
vocational potential. Referred to by
educators as occupational education.

WORK ADJUSTMENT   The modification of behavior and atti-
TRAINING   tudes and building up of work tolerance in a formal, usually institutional,
setting such as a sheltered workshop.

SHELTERED WORKSHOP   Means a rehabilitation facility which
affords a variety of controlled work
settings and experiences similar to
those in competitive industry through
which professional rehabilitation personnel provide vocational evaluation,
work adjustment training services, rehabilitation counseling and other related services to handicapped people
in an individualized program. The
goal of a sheltered workshop is the
placement of these handicapped people in jobs in competitive industries,
or if this is not feasible, in sheltered
employment in the workshop.

REHABILITATION CENTER   Means a rehabilitation facility offering
a coordinated range of restorative and
adjustive services under one management for the purpose of assisting
handicapped people toward a productive, contributing role in the community. Such services usually include
most of the following: medical evaluation, medical management, physical
therapy, occupational therapy, speech
and hearing services, psychiatric, psychological, and social services, voca-

tional counseling, vocational evaluation, vocational training, sheltered workshop services, and job placement and follow-up.

WORK ACTIVITIES CENTER

Means a workshop or a physically separated department of a workshop having an identifiable program, separate supervision and records, planned and designed exclusively to provide therapeutic activities for handicapped workers whose physical or mental impairment is so severe as to make their productive capacity inconsequential.

VOCATIONAL GOAL

A specific employment objective for an individual client based on *his* aptitudes, interest, and needs, using all available information concerning the client.

PRE-VOCATIONAL
EVALUATION

Usually in a formal setting, the gathering of pertinent information necessary to set a vocational goal. Includes specific aptitudes, work tolerance, and attitude.

The fact-gathering process *in toto*. Securing medical, psychological and social information. This may include a pre-vocational evaluation in a formal setting.

COUNSELING

Interpersonal relationship with a client in which he is assisted to adjust to himself and his environment more effectively. In the vocational rehabilitation setting it is *not* meant to be of a deep therapeutic nature.

A PLAN

(1) A cohesive statement in a case record of the medical, psychological, vocational, and social factors in order to justify a rehabilitative process or expenditure. (2) A statement of spe-

cifics. That is, how, when, and to whom an expenditure is to be made. It must be approved by a supervisory person and a medical or psychological consultant when indicated.

AUTHORIZATION

A *written* agreement to pay for a *specific* service from a *specific* contractor. It must be given *prior* to the provision of service in order to make payment.

SURVEY

An initial or intake interview during which a rehabilitation counselor obtains an employment and education history as well as information concerning medical treatment and social background.

ASSIGNED

When an application is received in a local office the rehab agency gives it to a particular counselor based on geographic area and/or disability grouping. This does *not* mean that the case has been accepted.

ACCEPTED
(Active)

Based on the diagnostic information gathered by the counselor, he is able to dictate a formal statement into the record that a client meets the eligibility requirements mentioned above.

RETURN

Physical or mental improvement of function that is attributed to treatment (versus natural return).

EXTENDED
EVALUATION

If, during the diagnostic process for a disabled, *handicapped* client, a counselor cannot determine vocational potential well enough to:

1. Declare the client eligible,
2. Declare him ineligible,

he may provide services on a trial basis to help make this determination. This may be considered an evaluation technique, although many of the same services are given as in the regular program. As soon as the client can be, with surety, declared eligible or ineligible he must be removed from this program (also must be removed at the end of 6 or 18 months depending on disability).

CONSULTANT
(Medical and
Psychiatric)

A medical doctor who approves a plan of action as being *medically* correct. This includes psychiatric work. He also is used to answer questions concerning problems prior to treatment programs.

SPECIALTY EXAMINATION

A medical examination by a doctor who has specialized in a given field, e.g., cardiac, orthopedic, ophthalmic, otiatric, and so on.

CASE RECORD

In the state rehabilitation program it is made up of essentially three parts—reports (medical, etc.), correspondence, and a narrative of case activity by the counselor.

INELIGIBLE

The failure to meet one or more of the eligibility criteria, i.e., not "disabled," not limited, or so severely limited so as to preclude vocational placement.

CLOSURE

A formal statement in the case record giving the reasons why a case is being removed from active files of the agency. Generally approved by a supervisory person.

1. Early in case development if the client is found ineligible, if he cannot be contacted, expresses disinterest, etc.
2. If the client has received services to no avail.

3. After services have led to successful placement.

A "REHABILITATION"

A person who has been through the
rehabilitation process and is successfully employed. Frequently referred
to as "rehab" and the person, more
formally, called a rehabilitant.

18

Advocacy: A Struggle for Power

by Douglas P. Biklen

What happens if . . .

(Case 1)
You are told by your local school officials that your child cannot attend school because he is "inappropriate" for the classes available?

(Case 2)
Your son has been excluded from public school, you place him in a state school for the retarded only to find that he is beaten and then subsequently transferred to a prison?

(Case 3)
You have two children who are in junior high and high school and who have been excluded from school off and on throughout their school careers because they have profound hearing losses

(deafness) and because the schools are less than enthusiastic about providing special services?

(Case 4)

Your son has been denied public education for most of his school-age years and because you cannot find any community services for him and you are unable to care for him on a full-time basis in your own home, you have to place him in an institution for the "retarded" where you find that he loses many of the skills and self-care habits that he had learned at home?

These cases represent what has actually happened to four families and, most certainly, what has happened to many parents and children across the country. Far from bizarre and unusual, these cases accurately portray the problems of more than a few isolated children. Over one million school-age youths do not attend school. Further, the number of people under age twenty-one who have been institutionalized is probably over 200,000, this figure extrapolated from the nearly 600,000 people (adults and children) in state schools for the retarded and state mental hospitals. A still more convincing bit of evidence that youths do not receive all the educational and other training services that they require lies in the number of right-to-treatment suits developed throughout the United States. Most important among these legal actions have been the right-to-treatment cases for the institutionalized (Partlow State School and Willowbrook State School) and right-to-education suits, most notably in Washington, D.C., and Pennsylvania.°

In order for the reader to more fully understand the responses of parents and their children to such conditions as have been

° *Wyatt* v. *Stickney*, 344 F. Supp. 387, 390 (1972); *Parisi et al.* v. *Rockefeller et al.*, C.A. No. 72-C-356, Decree (April 10, 1973); *Mills* v. *Board of Education*, C.A. No. 1939–71, Decree (D.D.C., August 1, 1972); *Pennsylvania Association for Retarded Children* v. *Pennsylvania*, 343 Supp. 279, 297 (E.D. Pa. 1972).

described in the four cases, I will provide additional details from each case. (All names have been changed to protect the privacy of those involved.)

First, Mr. and Mrs. Capere took their son, who was and is blind, to attend the kindergarten of their local school. As Mr. Capere later explained, "I got a real education from this. I am the kind of guy who works hard. I'm a machinist." As he spoke, he raised his grit-filled fingernails to show that indeed he was a worker. "I go to work in the morning and I come home in the late afternoon. That's how I live my life. But now I don't know. I got a rude awakening through all of this. Maybe some things need some changing. I'm not scared of speaking out any longer. You see, I'm a Frenchman and I have a temper. Well, my son wasn't at school for two days and the principal calls, angry as anything, and says, 'I didn't know your son was blind. We don't have any programs for him here. Why didn't you tell me? He's not appropriate for our classes. You'll have to take him out today.'" As Mr. Capere explained, "I was like the donkey that the farmer had to hit over the head with a fence rail to get his attention before explaining the day's work." Mr. Capere felt stunned by the principal's swift exclusion order against his five-year-old son. "What did 'inappropriate' mean?" Mr. Capere asked.

The Caperes were advised to apply to the regional institution for the blind, operated by the state. However, their son was not accepted by this school on the grounds that he was "mentally retarded" as well as blind. Then began a long search for schooling that lasted for eight more years, until their son was of junior-high-school age. Meanwhile, he was not accepted at any private schools, neither in their own state, nor in another state. Further, the Caperes were offered no assistance by the local district in finding services. When they asked for help from the state commission on the visually handicapped, that commission offered a list of possible schools to which their son might apply. None of these worked out. On one occasion, a private school wrote back to the Caperes and suggested that they contact the commission on the visually impaired. The Caperes felt the circular message: Private schools referred them back to the state-operated school for the blind in their own region.

Finally, after seven years of searching, Mr. and Mrs. Capere returned with their son to the state residential program. Here they were told that the school would not accept their son because he had received no formal schooling in the last seven years! It was only when school tests revealed his intelligence to be normal and his aptitude to be relatively high that the school finally agreed to accept him into its program. By this time the Caperes had become aware of their legal right under the state education laws and constitution to demand a publicly supported education program for their son. Once they could demand these services, they no longer had to beg for them as if they were a privilege for which a person had to qualify.

This successful end to a long struggle came at the same time that a federal court judge was ruling on a case in Washington, D.C., that *all* children (regardless of their disabilities) had a right to an education and that even if funds were limited, the handicapped could no longer be denied an education. The judge ruled:

> If sufficient funds are not available to finance all of the services and programs that are needed in the system then the available funds must be expended equitably in such a manner that no child is entirely excluded from a publicly supported education consistent with his needs and ability to benefit therefrom.

The second case involved a boy, aged sixteen, who had been institutionalized by his parents in a school for the retarded when he was only five years old. As with the Caperes' son, he too was excluded from the local public school. Young Dennis Edwards had been beaten (he had bruises and cuts on his back and head) just prior to a holiday when the Edwards family intended to take him home for a short stay. Mr. Edwards explained to me that the institution had discouraged visits by the family and had not allowed them to view Dennis's living quarters. The Edwardses never received reports on their son's progress. When they found that he had been beaten, they made inquiries of other children at the institution. Dennis's friends reported that he had been beaten by an attendant. Mr. and Mrs. Edwards quickly notified an attorney who initiated a large damage suit against the state officials. Unfortunately, the attendant who had allegedly been involved in the beating was never identified by the institutional officials and, after a period of legal hearings, the case fell apart. A few weeks later, when the case was in a state of disrepair, the state school staff sent a letter to the Edwardses explaining that their son would be transferred to another institution. When Mr. and Mrs. Edwards arrived at the new institution, they were informed that Dennis now resided in a prison facility; he occupied a small steel cell, replete with a steel prison bunk and a small toilet and washbasin. The state school had managed to obtain a court order for Dennis's transfer into the prison on the grounds that he was "a dangerous male in a state school."

When Mr. and Mrs. Edwards inquired as to the cause of Dennis's incarceration in a prison, one guard explained to them, "What do you mean? He's like the rest. Caught for using drugs." Dennis was apparently so heavily tranquilized by the state school staff that when he arrived at the prison he was assumed to be a drug user from the "streets," at least by those guards who had not seen his records. It was later discovered that for eight years he had been given a drug to control seizures, even though he had no record of seizures.

Finally, Mr. and Mrs. Edwards sought assistance from a child-advocacy group that was able to obtain a court order to permit them to visit Dennis and to assess the situation. It was determined that he was receiving no educational program and that he was "dangerous" only when taunted by other inmates. With another court order, the advocacy group was able to secure his transfer back to his home community, where he currently attends a day program and lives on weekends with his family. In contrast to the prognosis of the institutional staff that he was dangerous and extremely limited, Dennis has demonstrated an ability to participate in community life; among other things, he is able to go to the neighborhood grocery store to buy household items, he attends church with his family, and he mows lawns in the neighborhood.

The Edwardses still face the problem of finding adequate and useful training programs for Dennis. While he progresses satisfactorily in the community, he still lacks structured programming that would enable him to become more self-sufficient. In order to meet these needs, the Edwardses began to organize with other parents and citizens in the community.

The third case involved two children with severe hearing impairment who, like the previous youths, were excluded from public school. For several years, the Jackson family faced imminent exclusion from school of their eldest son, Michael. A letter came from the director of special education in their school district; it revealed the pressure on them to withdraw Michael from the local school and to place him in a residential facility far from their home:

> It is my unpleasant duty to inform you that your son is being accepted into the hard of hearing class for this school year only. We hope that you have seriously reviewed our recommendation of June 8, 1966.

Michael's teacher explained to Mrs. Jackson, "I know you don't want to send him to an institution, but he's incapable of learning so he should be with other people like himself so he would have their companionship." When Mrs. Jackson responded by saying that he seemed to be making excellent progress in the schools, with A's in spelling, for example, the teacher responded, "I think you're making a big mistake putting him into the public schools." Later a school counselor threatened legal action to force the Jacksons to institutionalize their son.

Finally, the Jacksons received the exclusion order for both children:

> Enclosed are the completed exemption certificates for Cindy and Michael Jackson in accordance with Section 3208 of the Education Law and Article XXX, Sections 230–235, of the regulations of the Commissioner of Education.

When the Jacksons continued to disobey the exclusion order, the principal of their school ordered the bus dispatcher to bar the children from entering the school bus. At this point, other children in the school developed a petition calling on school officials to permit the children to remain in the public schools, despite the lack of special education programming.

When the Jacksons called for a meeting before the local school board, with a crowd of other interested parents and citizens flooding the board meeting room to watch the proceedings, the school officials began to give some ground. They conceded to allow the Jackson children to attend the public school. The superintendent said, "We will accept the children if you will agree to accept the responsibility of educating them." Mr. and Mrs. Jackson agreed to this concession in order to keep their children at home, but before long, Mrs. Jackson began to organize parents of deaf children in her district behind a movement to force the schools to hire a certified teacher of the deaf. The parents became their own advocates by publicizing their legal rights to have such a teacher for their children. Further, the parents informed the school officials that failure to respond to their needs would constitute a breach of state law and could possibly be met with legal action by a nearby public-interest child-advocacy group. Under mounting pressure, secured by the parents through their own demonstration of strength at school board meetings, and through press coverage both on television and in the newspapers, the school district hired a teacher of the deaf.

The fourth case concerned another youth, David, who was institutionalized at the Willowbrook State School for the Mentally Retarded. When David's treatment at Willowbrook was found lacking and, in fact, negative to his development, his parents joined a federal lawsuit on behalf of all the children at the Willowbrook institution. The law brief read as follows:

> Plaintiff David, aged twelve, resides at Willowbrook in Building 76, Ward 2. He was admitted in August of 1970. There are 35 other children on his ward. During the day his ward is staffed by one or two attendants. At night there is frequently only one attendant.

> David attended public school facilities for one or two hours per day from age 7 to age 10. School officials then told David's parents that he could no longer attend public school facilities, though they were not told why, and that if they did not take David out of public school he would be "kicked out." David's parents were unable to care for him at home, on a permanent basis, and tried unsuccessfully to find another school or a community facility.

> Subsequently, David's parents were told by a social worker in the Metropolitan Hygiene Retardation Clinic, the screening agency for the Department of Mental Hygiene, that he was too old to be admitted to Willowbrook and would not be admitted unless they consented to place him in the experimental hepatitis research program, which they reluctantly did.[2]

David was transferred to two other buildings after he went through the hepatitis program. His parents insisted that he be given schooling and he was later placed in a school program.

[2] *Parisi et al.* v. *Rockefeller et al.* C.A. No. 72-C-356.

But after a few weeks the teacher suspended him because he had started to soil himself. Before David entered Willowbrook he was toilet trained. But now, when his parents bring him home, they find he wets his bed. After much effort, David's mother got him back in a Willowbrook school program, but only for one hour every afternoon.[3]

David's parents complained about the general living quarters:

The children on David's ward all sleep in one long room. There are a few chairs and a television set, but no rugs, lamps, pictures, games, books, or toys.[4]

The federal lawsuit was an attempt to remedy these conditions.

Seize Power

How can families respond to conditions such as those we have described in the four cases? How do you react to the pronouncement that your son or daughter is inappropriate for public school programs? What can you do when your child is placed in various settings without your approval, as in the case involving Dennis's transfer to a prison? How can you challenge the forceful exclusion of your children from the public schools? How can you change the Willowbrooks of our society?

What I will suggest in this chapter is that the answer, if there can be an answer to such problems, will not be found in further clinical study of the various disabilities such as deafness, mental retardation, visual impairments, and learning disabilities, but rather in the society as a whole. There currently exists no scientific evidence that children benefit more from institutionalization, from education in segregated schools, or from special education in the regular schools. Far from being questions that

---

[3] *Idem.*
[4] *Idem.*

scientists should bother with, these are political and moral questions that must be answered in accordance with our visions of what the society is to become. If we choose to treat people with disabilities as surplus populations, then we may well choose to segregate and institutionalize the children mentioned in the four cases. If, on the other hand, we decide that ours will be an open society where all members are valued as fellow human beings, then we will have little reason to isolate and segregate.

As each of the four cases demonstrates, people can change the current trends toward dehumanization and isolation of people with handicaps only by creating power and by withdrawing support from those official decisions and practices that dehumanize or exclude children. To cite one example that parallels each of the four cases above, school principals may exclude or exempt children whom they label as "inappropriate" or "severely disabled" only so long as they have the cooperation and obedience of other professionals and parents, and so long as they can argue convincingly that it is the children who must "fit" into the school rather than vice versa. When parents withdraw their approval from such actions, when parents seek to bring legal actions against school districts, and when other professionals begin to reject policies of exclusion as professionally irresponsible and immoral, the principal stands on shakier ground.

When parents organize themselves for action, they demonstrate that power is no bureaucracy's monopoly. Rather, a few people in the society or in a particular area of life—for example, the schools and institutions—exercise considerable power because others cooperate with and obey them. As the Jacksons demonstrated when they organized other parents, the power of policymakers depends on support and acquiescence from a constituency. Similarly, a group of professionals in society were formerly free to label children according to a variety of disability categories, to exclude children from school, to demand institutionalization, and to forgo treatment or service of children. All of these policies have been challenged both through community organizing of parents, through dissension within professional ranks, and, most important, by a series of lawsuits (e.g., *Pennsylvania Association for Retarded Children* v. *Commonwealth of Pennsylvania; Mills* v. *Board of Education; Wyatt* v. *Stickney*). There was a time, which may still be with us to some extent, when many parents were reluctant to confront the schools and institutions because they (the parents) regarded educational services as a privilege. This has changed. Parents are now demanding justice; they recognize that their sons and daughters have a "right to an equal education," regardless of their disability.

Community Organizing: The Uses of Power

Parents must learn to give and withdraw their support from officials who deal with disabled youth; that is, parents must learn to use power themselves. The conclusion of this chapter will provide strategies toward those ends.

The steps that lead to and effect change can be categorized in three levels: analysis; action; securing the change. The first step requires parents and other organizers to develop an understanding of themselves and their values and goals, an identification of community problems, a process of building alliances with others, and an understanding of how the desired changes will be resisted.

Understanding yourself, your biases, your values, and your goals means that you must begin to define what is important to you. In each of the cases presented earlier, parents found themselves reacting to policies and practices of officials who came in contact with their children. Yet all of the parents knew

that they were not satisfied with what was happening to their
children. In each case, the parents had their own private vision
of what they wanted for their sons or daughters. It was this
personal vision that enabled them to seek alternatives. These
parents questioned the labeling of their children, the placement
procedures that affected their children, the subjective decisions,
e.g., labeling the children as inappropriate or ineligible for
certain programs, and the isolation of their children into
institutions. Clearly, their ability to challenge decisions that had
been made about their children stemmed at least in part from
their strong desires to have their children live in a community,
to interact with other typical children, to receive programs that
would help their children develop. These parents were not
willing to view education and other treatment programs as
privileges but rather insisted that their children had rights to
such services. As Mr. Edwards put it, "They never did anything
for my son. They never gave him an education. We want him to
have an education."

The identification of community problems grew out of what
these four sets of parents saw happening to their own children.
In each case, the parents realized that their own problems were
linked to the problems of other parents and their children. The
Edwardses saw that all the other children in the state school
ward where their son resided were also not receiving adequate
services. In the case of David, the parents joined with other
parents in bringing a class action (on behalf of all youths in
similar situations at Willowbrook) lawsuit against the state for
inadequate care and treatment. Similarly, the Jacksons realized
that there were other children in their county who were deaf
and who, as a result of school policies, were forced out of the
public schools and into the single alternative, the residential
schools for deaf children. With other parents, the Jacksons
participated in a survey of parents of deaf children and found
that the problems they experienced were also faced by over fifty

other children. A second survey carried out by another group of parents revealed over a hundred deaf children who had been denied local educational programs. Even the Caperes, who lived in a rural area, found that children with other disabilities had been denied local school programs in their district. As the parents began to ask questions on behalf of their own children they each uncovered broader problems throughout the community. The problems were inadequate and exclusionary local services, institutionalization, and dehumanization in institutions.

Many of the parents looked to find allies in the service agencies that had failed to serve their children. In each case, they found some staff who were sympathetic. Yet none of them found adequate solutions forthcoming. They had to turn to other parents and consumers who had experienced similar problems. They had to seek out professionals who did not work in the schools and institutions where they were finding such resistance; they had to find professionals who did not have a self-interest in perpetuating the policies that needed changing. These groups of nonaligned professionals and fellow parents or consumers became their allies in the push for better services.

Finally, they had to examine how the schools and institutions were able to resist change. They found a variety of strategies or practices that seemed to serve as barriers to change. For one thing, they found that the institutions often explained away the lack of programming by arguing that they were simply short of staff (an apparently frequent excuse) or that they were just developing new programs, programs that somehow never materialized. In several instances parents encountered fancy phrases that supposedly describe ongoing programs, but which actually serve to mask questionable activities: the term "milieu therapy" refers to sitting around on the wards; the term "occupational therapy" refers to arts and crafts rather than real job training. In the public schools they found their children were excluded on the grounds that they were too "severely disabled." It was never explained why adequate programs could not be developed for severely disabled children. In several instances the parents found themselves characterized by school and institutional officials as too emotional and too involved: "Don't worry about it. You must learn to accept your child's best interest." Another strategy that prevailed in the schools and institutions was testing and labeling. The diagnostic processes served to place blame for nonservice on the children by labeling their needs as "severe" and hence requiring institutionalization. Yet institutions were not responding to these severe needs. At one institution, a child who was receiving no services at all was criticized as violent and uncontrollable. The blame was placed on the child rather than on the institution.

The second step, action, involves only one major element: choosing and implementing strategies of change that are consistent with what the parents want to achieve and which, most important, will be successful. The parents in the case examples learned, as all organizers must, that they had to fashion their actions to their needs and that they could not afford to spend their energies on strategies that would certainly fail. Their actions included demonstrations at school board meetings, press conferences by other parents and themselves, demands to school officials, and the threat of lawsuits to establish their children's rights. In each case, the least victory that the parents would win was a basic education of the entire community to the problems that they and their children faced.

Other tactics that have proved useful include statements at public hearings, negotiation with bureaucracies, picketing, leafleting, letter writing, the creation of model programs to demonstrate the viability of an alternative, and lobbying.

Often, consumers—in this case the consumers are parents—choose a single tactic as the "best and only answer" to their problems. I have often been asked, for example, "Don't you think lobbying is the answer? Isn't legislative change essential?"

No, lobbying is not an answer; it is just a tactic, one of many. In order to seek basic policy changes that will improve the opportunities of youth, parents and other advocates usually need a variety of tactics suited to particular circumstances. In many cases, for example, laws already exist to protect the rights of people with disabilities, yet because of social prejudices or simply "red tape," bureaucracies such as school districts or institutions may fail to fulfill the mandate of law. Such circumstances require tactics other than lobbying, such as demonstrations, demands, and threats of legal action. If a group of youths has been denied a full educational program, for example, parents may be able to remedy the situation through a well-organized series of "media events" and through a rather traditional tactic such as letter writing. Parent groups can write "open letters" to agency officials, with carbon copies to attorneys and to local newspaper editors and reporters. If the letters are sent "registered" or "certified," officials may respond quickly for fear that a legal record is being developed by the parents to document the illegal or, at least, questionable policies of the agency. This strategy may succeed, but if it fails to elicit an adequate response, the parents may choose to hold a press conference where they can present a series of demands. Then the officials must respond publicly to newspaper, radio, and television reporters. Parents can continue to intensify public pressure on officials through an ongoing campaign of events that draw repeated media coverage; these may include picketing, public attempts to register their sons and daughters in educational programs (the newspapers and radio and television stations should be notified of these efforts in time for them to provide coverage), or appeals to higher public officials for complete inquiries into the problem. Finally, legal action (a lawsuit) remains in the background as a possible tactic for the consumers to utilize if all else fails.

In other words, consumers need to choose many tactics that

are both suited to their members' abilities to carry them through and which fit the circumstances. Further, since most problems cannot be solved with a single "action," consumers should prepare a series of events over a long period of time. One often hears the complaint, "I tried demonstrating and that didn't work, so what's the use of trying again?" If a single demonstration could solve most of the problems we face, few parents would feel powerless and pessimistic about the chances of changing the policies of human service agencies. And yet the experiences of those families cited in this chapter prove that when we link one tactic to another in a longer plan, parents' actions can replace their feelings of powerlessness with a sense of purpose and commitment to change.

Advocates can adopt any of the following tactics to promote the rights of people with disabilities:

Demonstrations

Demonstrations are a form of public communication that publicizes your issues and helps you monitor institutions, social service agencies, schools, and courts. Demonstrations, including marches, vigils, sit-ins, phone-ins, sing-ins, and picketing are a "community presence." Though for some the concept of a "demonstration" holds the feelings of violence on college campuses in the 1960s, they are nevertheless a viable, legal medium.

Demands

When a group makes demands, it tells the whole community that people who have disabilities also have rights. In a society which has encouraged people with disabilities to seek charity or favors, the process of making demands can change attitudes. Demands may be stated as a bill of rights or as a list of grievances.

Letter Writing

When people think of letter writing they think of the "letter to a Congressman." Actually, letter writing can include other effective forms: carbon copies to attorneys; public letters; leaflets at community centers or shopping centers; letters to editors; skywriting; newsletters; letter bulletins; letters of support to groups or people who share your interests; and letters of complaint. And letters can serve to create a formal record of your efforts to seek services.

Public Hearings and Fact-Finding Forums

Fact-finding panels or public hearings can help identify community needs, but they can also serve as an action. Any citizen can give testimony (usually five or ten minutes' worth) before legislative panels, town councils, and county legislatures. When people give testimony in any of these forums, they throw their concerns into public view; they make their own personal troubles into public issues that demand public solutions.

Community Education

In order to change policies, we must first change attitudes. Parent groups and advocates throughout the country have used booklets, pamphlets, seminars, workshops, slide shows, movies, resource guides, press conferences, TV debates, radio shows, exposés, phoning campaigns, advertisements, public service announcements, and press releases. Communications help to educate your supporters and the broader community.

Symbolic Acts

Symbolic acts, including mock awards, mock elections, and mock public hearings, call attention, often sarcastically, to a policy, practice, or need that deserves exposure. Because it appears shocking or unusual, the symbolic act is talked about long after the action has occurred.

Negotiation

In every type of advocacy, there will be times when confrontation is not needed, when you can negotiate for the concessions you desire. You can use negotiations as a way of finding out where the bureaucracy stands. In some instances, you may want your own experts, lawyers, or other parents to assist in your negotiations.

Lobbying

Lobbying may mean pushing for legislative or administrative policy change. You can use several tactics, including phone calls, petitions, alternative budgets and alternative plans, telegram campaigns, and public statements. Aside from the ultimate goal of legislative change, lobbying also educates legislators and the public, it solidifies large numbers of parents behind agreed-upon goals, and it helps the lobbyist become better informed.

Boycotts

Sometimes, a short boycott (one week, perhaps) can prove so embarrassing to the bureaucracy that you may win your objectives. As with other tactics, the boycott helps to publicize your needs and concerns. During the boycott, you may want to establish an alternative service (for example, a school) to the service that you have chosen to boycott.

The opposite of boycott is a work-in or persistent demands for service. Parents, for example, may refuse to leave a service agency until their children are served.

Model Programs

If you can demonstrate workable alternatives to current service systems, people will begin to think of change as practical and possible. The creation of alternative social institutions often forces existing institutions to change.

Legal Action

Lawsuits, legal memoranda, legal rights booklets, legal representations for parents on behalf of their sons and daughters have all become permanent parts of advocacy. Whenever you seek basic services such as education, be sure to learn your legal rights.

Each of these procedures involves the public and communication. A head-on confrontation between parents and administrators exclusive of outside support or mediation means less support and participation from other groups with similar interests. Parents may feel that holding a work-in or a demonstration is going overboard or acting childishly, but they are legitimate methods of resolving conflicts.

The Jackson case portrays how a family was able to push for their goals through a series of strategies, each of which went a step further than the other. They began their struggle by individually refusing to withdraw their children from school and by initiating a community survey of the overall problem of deaf children. Next, they corresponded with their state legislators; further, they organized a meeting before the local school board that included a show of strength by interested neighbors. When they accepted the superintendent's offer to admit the children into school for "socialization only," they agreed to these terms temporarily, but they remained active in the search for a more adequate solution. The Jacksons formed a lobbying group comprised of parents of disabled children. This group began to make demands on the school district which were consistent with their rights as they were defined in the state education law. The coverage by local newspapers of their group's activities added to the pressure on local school officials to meet their needs. Finally, when a nearby parents group, larger than their own, began to discuss the possibility of legal action on behalf of all deaf children in the county, the Jacksons' district moved ahead and hired a certified teacher.

The third and final step for the Jacksons and for all parents who initiate action on behalf of their children is to make the change permanent. In the case of Dennis Edwards, for example, who had been released from the prison and transferred back to a program in his community, the Edwardses decided to keep in close touch with other parents of children in his same program, a step that was facilitated by a sensitive staff member in the program. As Dorothea Dix wrote in 1843, "abuses assuredly cannot always or altogether be guarded against," but each of us can become constant advocates. In short, the best insurance against recurring abuses is to remain involved, to maintain contact with your allies, and to keep an eye on community problems. In this sense, the only way to make change permanent is to share your success with others, advertise it, and continue to work for change. A relatively recent tactic has been the banding together of cross-disability groups—parents of the mentally retarded, deaf, blind, learning disabled, emotionally disturbed, and physically disabled together—which is creating a power bloc and monitoring force. Unlike specific disability groups of years past, these cross-disability groups have begun to act on the belief that the problem is not a clinical or scientific one so much as it is a matter of community and professional attitudes. Parents of children with very different disabilities have begun to recognize their *common* problems. They have joined in common struggle.

Conclusion

Several recent landmark court actions have achieved several of the goals in this chapter—the right to education and the right to treatment. In Pennsylvania, the Association for Retarded Children sued the state in federal court on behalf of all retarded children of Pennsylvania for the right to public education. Plaintiffs in the Pennsylvania action were eleven so-called retarded children who for years had been denied educational opportunities and who had, heretofore, been segregated from their peers. This case was based on the right to due process (to fair hearings and questioning of policies) and to equal protection guarantees of the Fourteenth Amendment to the U.S. Constitution (that is, the same rights as others). The famous *Brown* v. *Board of Education* case was cited as a precedent for the right to equal education. In the presentation of the case before the federal judge, one witness explained that *all* children can learn and that all children should therefore have a right to an education. Since that initial landmark, lawyers and parents have filed over fifty similar right-to-education suits in twenty-two states for all school-age children, regardless of their disabilities. The most comprehensive of these suits, *Mills* v. *Board of Education of Washington, D.C.*, places considerable responsibility on school officials to justify any special placement or denial of education; according to the court order, parents are provided the opportunity to reject the school board's placement decisions.

Similar court actions have been brought on behalf of institutionalized children. The foremost case in Alabama resulted in a decision that youths in institutions had a right to decent treatment and, further, that no child could be placed in an institution unless it could be shown that he would not benefit from less confined programs (in public schools for example).

Each of these cases stands as a benchmark because each introduces the notion of rights of the disabled. They demonstrated that people need not quietly endure dehumanizing conditions. Yet the court cases will not provide ultimate solutions. The only ultimate answer to the problems raised here is a conscious use of power by parents and consumers in their day-to-day efforts to receive services. While the struggle may be assisted by these favorable court decisions and by an increasing acceptance in the society that people with disabilities have rights, the struggle itself, the conscious use of power, looms as our single best answer.

III

For
Professionals

19

Professional Uses and Abuses

In their diversity of diagnostic and general procedures, theoretical emphases, and management, professionals differ as widely as the handicapped they treat.

We might well ask ourselves, though, why there are so many points of view, why clients must "shop around" for the one that best suits them, and what the forces are that have influenced our profession. I suggest that many of the differences among us are based on "research" highlighting artificial situations. We often think of the brain injured as hyperactive, which may be the case in, say, the school where a youth may be responding to inappropriate teaching. Observed in the home, however, the child might sit passively for hours at the television or some card game. Few if any tests incorporate differences of stimuli into their evaluation. In addition, time limits are frequently imposed, an extension of our belief that "how fast" is more important than "how well."

Perhaps most damaging to child and parent is our emphasis on IQ, a great destroyer of personal confidence and ambition. Far more important are potential, number of friends, general sociability, and self-acceptance. Why interfere with these processes by introducing a block that is irrelevant to the handicapped person's performance and overall adjustment? Such artificial measurements of ability are sure to create even more problems, or false hopes in those whose IQ alone inspires them. Let more concrete aspects of the person's existence be the determinants of the kind of rehabilitative program that needs to be developed.

I'm also distressed by old-fashioned diagnostic categories and generalizations that lock parents into guilt complexes they don't need and clients into latencies that don't exist. When I was new in the profession, the popular latency was psychopathic personality—we've since progressed to homosexuality and schizophrenia. I like what Thomas Szasz says about schizophrenia: "If you talk to God, you are praying; if God talks to you, you have schizophrenia." * My own opinion on sexuality is that we're all bi-, hetero-, homo-, auto-, trans-, and trisexual (someone who tries everything). Latency, I conclude, is a figment of the psychiatric imagination. We might as well say that all women are latently pregnant.

I seldom use traditional tests in my own work, since simply going for a walk, out to lunch, or observing the person in a group situation gives me a more meaningful foundation for diagnosis. Testing often neglects the fact that a client is not an eye or an orthopedic problem or a reading disability, but is rather a whole person concerned with many priorities other than the handicap itself. I'll never forget a school for severely

* *The Second Sin* (New York: Anchor Books, 1974), p. 113.

handicapped young adults, with excellent services—a speech therapist, psychotherapist, hearing specialist, physical therapist —every imaginable special service. Yet, no attention was paid to personal needs of the handicapped, who were simply shuffled from professional to professional in an inflexible schedule tailored to the convenience of the therapist, not the client. Perhaps once a year a case conference was held for all therapists, but even here the "handicap" was stressed, not how well the person made friends, was he lonely or bored, did he accept himself.

There was, in fact, a failure to appreciate that this preoccupation with service complicated the condition of the person with a handicap. As detailed elsewhere, professionals seldom consider psychological readiness for services that may be altogether inappropriate or premature.

To illustrate: Some time ago I had reached the point where my ophthalmologist suggested I needed bifocals. Although I predicted I couldn't manage with them, he ridiculed my hesitation and insisted that with practice I would adjust like everyone else who ever wore them. Through my subsequent suffering he assured me that I'd have to be an idiot not to succeed. After three months of outright failure I finally sought another doctor who appreciated that some people—indeed, as he said, quite a few—can't adjust, and he promptly prescribed two pairs of glasses.

In choosing a given course of treatment, then, we must consider its impact and influence on the client as most important. Studying psychiatric services that divisions of vocational rehabilitation developed for the handicapped has, for instance, reinforced my personal prejudice against individual therapy for anyone whose main problem is lack of friends and socialization skills. I feel that no matter how much personal insight the client achieves, it is of little value if it doesn't help the person become more socially integrated.

We must also abandon our belief that we are treating one person, when what is really involved are brothers and sisters, parents, school associates, and the public in general. In this respect professionals sometimes have a hard time seeing the client and his parents as partners in the helping relationship. I suggest that if we viewed our clients as customers and operated under the rule that "the customer is always right," we would more readily build a good reputation *and* offer a more valuable service. This would mean, for example, understanding what might well be rational guilt and worry among parents instead of dismissing it with the least effective approach—"You'll get over it . . . grow out of it . . . don't worry!" If you think about it, when was the last time someone said to *you* "Don't worry" and *you* stopped? It is helpful to remember that irrational guilt and anxiety disorganize people, but rational guilt helps people get organized and more effective in helping themselves and others.

Most of us realize the family is important in guiding the handicapped. Whatever forces have shaped the person's confidence in his abilities, emotional and physical adjustment to his handicap, sociability, interest in living, and general self-image come mainly from parents as well as societal expectations and pressures.

Professionals are obliged to make clear to the clients and family what represents their best judgment, and should indicate whether they are expressing a clinical judgment based on experience, making a probable prediction, stating some professional speculation, or just using their intuition. This is not to say we should always play it safe by saying we are not sure. Those of us who have had a serious opportunity to examine the research in the field of handicapping conditions are aware of how much more we ourselves need to know.

Despite their intense emotional involvement, parents' intuition, insight, and understanding are quite often astute, and should be given fair consideration. If we refuse their suggestions and insights or brush them aside, they will distrust and resent us and very likely will seek help elsewhere. If their ideas are irrational, overprotective, or even hysterical, this too must be dealt with and at least partially resolved before attention directed at the handicapped is likely to be of much help. We had better be sure that what parents have to say isn't in fact valid, even though they may say it in a hysterical or emotional way. We have to work together, because not all parent solicitousness is due to guilt; not all child fears of doing things are due to overprotection. It isn't always the parents who are saying no or the child who is saying "I can't."

Nearly as important as the parents in the helping relationship are the teachers. What kind of people are they? Are they emotionally mature? Can they handle extreme situations? Can they teach individuals who have handicaps? Spend time with the teachers, discuss the student, and develop strategies for working toward common goals.

I know some adolescents who, regardless of whether or not they are handicapped, dislike their teachers. But mixed in with their typical complaints are likely to be some dissatisfactions meriting attention. We shouldn't be afraid to suggest a new teacher or classroom situation if the present one seems to be inhibiting or counterproductive. If we have developed a good rapport with the school administration, this will be possible.

I suspect that we professionals have our own built-in deficiencies, among them being a common tendency to exaggerate the importance of initial diagnosis. This is especially true in areas not clearly defined, as in the case of learning and emotional disabilities, brain injury, and developmental lags. We sometimes forget that the best diagnosis comes at the end of the "case," after a sound rehabilitative program has been put into practice.

Further, the client and his parents (and related people) must realize that a diagnosis doesn't solve any problems in itself, although it may be a good start. Often, especially in schools where interviews with teachers, the client, and his parents may be all that is required, the addition of batteries of tests may simply create an illusion of service. Often the diagnosis assumes the proportions of a "cure." Among handicapped adolescents I have evaluated, up to 90 percent of all their school testing and evaluations have been of little value or has been used ineffectively. The following is an example.

A learning-disabled adolescent of average intelligence was recommended for testing by his teachers because he was friendless and depressed, blocked in reading, very nervous, and an underachiever. Six months later after a rigorous series of tests, the school psychologist's astonishing findings reported that the boy was of average intelligence, blocked in reading, depressed, and nervous, and that there was a considerable gap between the boy's potential and achievement!

Even though psychological testing may be inaccurate and not prognostic, we can attempt to extract some helpful data from the results for the resolution of some problems. Here, the clients are entitled to a full disclosure of findings in the context that they may not represent a total picture. No professional should represent his findings to anyone else without the client's consent. This is an important ethical consideration that is violated too frequently. We are especially sensitive to the situation in light of the abuses of confidentiality that have emerged in government and industry. IBM, a central figure in communications and related research, has developed the following code from which we might benefit here:

Four Principles of Privacy

1. Individuals should have access to information about themselves in record-keeping systems. And there should be some procedure for individuals to find out how this information is being used.

2. There should be some way for an individual to correct or amend an inaccurate record.
3. An individual should be able to prevent information from being improperly disclosed or used for other than authorized purposes without his or her consent, unless required by law.
4. The custodian of data files containing sensitive information should take reasonable precautions to be sure that the data are reliable and not misused.

In my judgment, a school psychiatrist's or psychologist's report should not be accessible to anybody, including the principal, teachers, rehabilitation workers, or outside agencies, without the client's and/or parent's consent. Further, clients have the right to deny they have been treated elsewhere should they feel they received poor service and don't want it to interfere with or influence further evaluation. My concern here is that we professionals are too often loyal to each other instead of the clients.

As a psychotherapist and counselor for emotionally and learning disabled youth for twenty-five years, I know that it is not possible to like everyone you serve. Although like or dislike for a client should provide some personal insight, no professional should offer help to a handicapped person with whom he is uncomfortable and to whom he can't offer a full measure of service. A good way of judging this is by figuring out if you feel energized or exhausted by the encounter with the client. If the latter persists over a few meetings, one should seriously consider referring the client elsewhere. As professionals we have a lot to offer, but sometimes clients will be uncomfortable with us. On the other hand, a client with expectations of a "miracle worker" is admittedly unrealistic and we mustn't reinforce such expectations with promises we can't fulfill.

Another area that professionals need to be cautious about is reinforcing a sense of failure by too quickly suggesting that "You could do it if you tried" and pointing to successful cases, particularly of handicapped youth. In addition, the plaintive cries of "Why did this happen to me?" or "Why did God do this?" are not easily answered. My own response is often something like "It's certainly a big disadvantage to have a handicap, and to tell you the truth, nobody knows why it happened to you (and of course in most cases it's nobody's fault). Feeling sorry for yourself only compounds your disability." I try to be helpful by raising the question "Do you want to respond to the situation by fussing and crying and making others unhappy, which seems like a double punishment, or do you want to see what we can do to make the best of it?"

There can be some degree of encouragement for the handicapped, however, in knowing they are not alone and that others survive and work effectively despite their handicaps. The "success" stories that are most often influential are those on a small scale, such as peers and schoolmates, rather than big-time celebrities who seem out of reach to most people.

Sometimes we reassure people too quickly. As a supervisor for students in training as counselors, one of the most frequent mistakes I have noticed inexperienced professionals make is offering praise too frequently and/or inappropriately. This can make it difficult for a client to make objective judgments of when he or she is making real progress. In other words, there is a catch in praise.

I once visited a workshop for the physically handicapped that included arts and crafts and some actual vocational training. One young man was diligently painting and having all of his work lavishly praised by everyone who passed by. When he asked me what I thought of his work, I paused, viewed his paintings and told him, "I like this one, this isn't bad, but this and those over there are not good at all. You show some promise of being very creative." It wasn't fair for this person to be encouraged to believe everything he did was "magnificent."

If a client of mine asks at our first meeting, "Can I trust you?"

I reply, "No." The person may be astonished but adds, "But you're a psychologist, you're supposed to be trusted." Yet I respond, "Me you can't trust. What is all this instant trust about? We might not even like each other. Trust is something we have to earn. It should not be taken for granted. All meaningful interactions involve a certain amount of risk." I've yet to lose a client this way. In fact, most are intrigued by the prospect of a developing relationship and the risk involved.

In my own work I try to use the relationship with the client as a bridge to other relationships. I'm not beyond suggesting to clients, handicapped or otherwise, that the reason they have no friends is that they're boring. It's a lot more honest than the sometimes empty remarks that if they're friendly they'll make friends, or there are lots of people who would like them. Obviously, if we're going to be blunt, it must be in the context of readiness, trust, and a plan directed to overcome the obstacle.

The nature of a client's relationships with other people may be more significant to his growth and self-acceptance than anything else. Perhaps because of our own upbringing and values, we often avoid any mention of sexuality and relating sexually to others. Since we may be uncomfortable with our own sexuality, we risk creating similar attitudes in our clients. These feelings of insecurity for our intimate selves can be a burden for individuals who are already having identity problems.

Occasionally, a client's problem (sexual or otherwise) will make us uneasy because we don't feel at ease with it ourselves. A client who is sexually frustrated may benefit from the direct suggestion that he or she masturbate when they feel like it. Needless to say, the more open and comfortable professionals are, the greater the likelihood that our clients will feel free to discuss their intimate conflicts with us. Further, no professional should dismiss the possibility of counseling or therapy for himself or herself with another professional to work out his or her own hangups.

In a sense, the best role for a professional is to serve as an advocate for the client. At times he must be a coordinator, an intermediary, a proponent, as well as a therapist, effective role model, a sensitive listener, and perhaps best of all simply his or her friend: Someone he can count on not to perpetuate the lies and injustices encountered elsewhere.

Make it a point to ask your clients precisely what they are doing with their leisure time: Do they paint, read, play a musical instrument, associate with peers, or are they inclined to mope or sit stationary staring out a window or at a television set for hours?

There's nothing wrong with suggesting homework (an integral part of the discipline of the rational emotive school of psychotherapy). This could even involve directions to watch a particular TV program to broaden interest, to read a special magazine or comic book you want to discuss with him, and to arrange for yourself or someone else to take the client to an event or an encounter group, meditation, or self-assertive training program. Even at times when I've been very busy, some of the best therapeutic encounters have been when I've taken the time to have lunch or go somewhere with a client. The hundreds of human potential centers that have proliferated in recent years can be of great help as well.

One of the most difficult things for professionals to cope with is the failure of clients to follow advice or instructions. We must face the fact that if our expectations of people differ from their emotional preparedness, treatment will be ineffectual. We must first deal with the psychological aspects of individual readiness. It may be helpful to begin by explaining to the client that your suggestions may be difficult to follow, and why this may be so.

A seventeen-year-old boy injured in an automobile accident was told that if he was ever to walk again, it would be after years of intensive rehabilitation and physical therapy. He simply couldn't accept this at first, and cried that he wanted to walk *now*. After expressing our sympathy and understanding and maintaining that it was the best that could be done, our job was to motivate the boy from total despair so he would work effectively and organize himself around the training procedure. Even with something this crucial, it may be necessary to delay treatment.

Though a diet may be absolutely necessary for physical rehabilitation, once clients try to reduce their intake of food they may become very anxious and tense. Hence, an alternative to deal with the anxiety may be needed before success with the diet is achieved. This is no small matter, as I've known many people with handicaps—blind, deaf, or learning disabled, etc.—whose problem of overweight had become more serious than their so-called main handicap. Factors such as weight and personal appearance are indeed important. They are often principal aspects of the unattractiveness, lethargy, and overall poor self-image that limit socialization efforts until they are dealt with effectively.

We're not doing our job if we're only preparing the handicapped to be better students, sons or daughters, patients, or the like. We are students for but one fourth of our lives, dependent sons and daughters for hopefully the same amount of time (unless the handicap precludes independence), and patients only as long as necessary. What of postschool, postfamily, postpatient days? This great expanse of time is what we must prepare our clients for.

My message is that professionals cannot be dogmatic or prejudiced in adhering to established "proven" methods and need to consider clients on individual merits. I studied the reports on one hundred "hard core" handicapped adults at a rehabilitation center and in not one case did the professional record significant success. I suggested that the individual therapy be abandoned and replaced with group therapy and socialization programs. My suggestions were not approved or appreciated.

Numerous rules and regulations of this rehabilitation service prohibited any such maneuver. The rules were based on the profitable nature of the existing structure, which would suffer should the recommended changes be instituted, even on an experimental basis. Obviously, the professionals involved were mainly to blame, for they should not have offered services on a "take-it-or-leave-it" basis. There are, of course, instances where individual therapy is the best approach.

Finally, professionals who derive significant portions of their income from persons who have handicaps are obliged to coordinate their efforts with other professionals, parents, and socialization groups to improve existing services. This may include volunteering to serve in advisory capacities in parent and advocacy groups, keeping in mind that we should not take control of such organizations. Although it may be appropriate to be the executive director, we should be sensitive in considering ourselves as employees of some governing board. Parents have the right to control their own organizations despite our best intentions.

Professional colleagues of mine who have been most helpful to handicapped people have not hesitated to use their influence in going out of their way to organize programs and activities for the handicapped. Let me illustrate several ideas and projects that have had great success.

Arranging for two people to meet who are clients.

Helping organize a Saturday recreation program.

Serving as a consultant for a socialization group.

Developing group counseling and guidance sessions for parents.

Working with the special education department of a local

college and organizing big-brother-type relationships
between students and people with handicaps (field work,
independent study, internships, experience credit).

Sponsoring special olympics.

Working in or with summer camps.

Developing organized travel projects to broaden experience and perspective.

Professionals need to go beyond their good intentions and the
payoff derived from good credentials and join with parents and
their colleagues to serve in an increasing advocacy role. Perhaps
even acknowledge that certain administrative changes in
schools, institutions, and social attitudes may be more important
than anything we have to offer right now. This doesn't mean we
don't have anything to offer. It just means that we must be open
to new methods which will offer clients the best possible care,
even if preexisting standards must be eliminated.

The helping relationship must involve more than talking
things over. In closing, I salute the many hundreds of professionals who have given tremendous time, energy, and expertise
in working with parent groups and developing seminars and
projects without compensation, whose motivation was essentially that of helping.

20

The School Scene:
Selected Short Subjects

I

Most teachers who are familiar with the job of teaching people who have handicaps will agree that new and better methods are required. Adjustments are needed in the amount of individual attention each student receives. Several states have begun programs to facilitate integration into regular classes whenever possible, endorsing our belief that socialization skills are better experienced than vicariously learned.

The crisis of remediation remains a national scandal among our schools. When confronted with a student experiencing difficulty in, say, reading, we conclude that what this person really needs is extra reading assignments. So we take a student who hates to read for fifteen minutes and we force him to read for an hour and a half.

In the case of reading, we sometimes fail to realize that there are many reasons for the difficulty. Often the problem extends beyond the learning disability, brain damage, visual impairment, or whatever originally caused it. If reading skills have been inappropriately demanded or expected of a child, he or she may become anxious and resentful of these unrealistic requirements. In other instances, bad learning experiences are due to loneliness and inferiority feelings, creating an apathetic attitude toward self-development, which may seem pointless. Thus, many students develop a block against reading, and any attempts to teach it, regardless of the method used, will not be successful until the block is resolved.

It is not difficult to teach a motivated student how to read or do arithmetic. If the basic interest and desire to learn is there, then the only problems may be in surmounting physical limitations. Among unmotivated and blocked readers, however, direct remediation efforts are often a waste of time, for they attempt to "unblock a block with a block." This is true of any problem subject.

Instead of forcing the issue, I advise teachers and parents to ease off for a while. It may be far more important for the child to develop some self-confidence in other areas before retackling something tainted with one failure after another. We need to assure students that the experiences they are going to have will not all be humiliating or failures.

Begin by teaching fantasy in your classes! Give assignments where any response is acceptable and there is an infinite variety of right answers. Once the students feel they have been given the opportunity to express themselves and that these expressions are healthy and good to develop, the imposed routine invariably becomes less of a threat to the student's identity.

II

Overdoses of competitiveness, long a trademark of our schools, may stifle your students, including those with handicaps. I can't tell you how many young people there are who could never learn to swim because they were learning it in a competitive situation; how ashamed many students have been when the teacher read the test scores out loud. Many young people could never learn to ride a bicycle because they were being taught by their older brother and people in the street were watching; who couldn't bowl in a regular bowling alley, and so on. In these and many other instances, common sense might tell us that a little extra confidentiality between student and teacher at first might be of benefit until the student feels comfortable about his or her abilities.

This is especially true of unmotivated students who may not (at least in public) care where they stand in school. At times, developing a good rapport and relationship with these students can build a desire to please the teacher and develop pride in the self. Homework should be reserved essentially for motivated students, since uninterested pupils very seldom profit from it.

III

One of the best antidotes for boredom is to learn something new. If your class is obviously uninterested during social studies, instead of doggedly pursuing the lesson to its close, stop and teach something new. If you're going to show slides or a movie, make sure it's interesting since otherwise many will fall asleep in the dark. Talk about outer space, life on other planets, latest discoveries, or leave it up to your students to bring up topics to teach each other.

IV

Many pupils, particularly those who haven't adjusted well to school life, equate education with submission. Conforming to the demands of teachers and administrators may symbolize relinquishing their remaining identity to a system they hate and don't understand. Young people are very sensitive to the vibrations and treatment they receive once they are labeled as deviant.

V

Depending on the nature of the disability, handicapped students in your classes may be more likely to do poorly academically, to act up in and out of class, and to be rejected socially. This can be a burden for the student, teacher, and peers if the situation is allowed to get out of hand with no attempt at communication and control.

There are some methods of communication that are obviously ineffective. Humiliating a student in front of a class is more likely to stimulate unacceptable behavior and dislike for you than prevent it. Deliberately calling on a student who is chronically unprepared, whose hand isn't raised, and who probably can't answer only strengthens the student's belief that he is dumb. A well-adjusted student may not mind having to stammer that he doesn't know, but a handicapped person's identity is more vulnerable.

We are not saying that established methods are necessarily undesirable. It seems apparent, however, that unless the pace, sequence, and emphasis are tailored somewhat to accommodate individual handicaps or difficulties, the process of not learning becomes an exhausting experience for both student and teacher.

VI

What is taught will have a great effect on how it is received. It must have been a historic moment a few years ago when publishers and curriculum developers got together and decided that "the reason we are not teaching children to read and write is because the curriculum is not relevant," and everybody stood up and applauded.

So they made Dick and Jane urban, black, and relevant, although Spot remained integrated, and I suspect that not a single black, Puerto Rican, Mexican-American, handicapped, or mentally retarded student learned to read as a result of the new curriculum. As a matter of fact, almost every large city in this country continues to report a decline of reading and arithmetic scores despite millions of dollars poured into remediation.

If you want to help, spread a rumor that "relevance is boring." If you say it is a fact, nobody will believe you. Everybody knows and loves Dr. Seuss, and Dr. Seuss is irrelevant. He makes up his own words and his own fantasies. Many educators are also fiercely jealous of *Sesame Street*. People who watch *Sesame Street* say they are watching it only because of their children. *Sesame Street* is irrelevant. Oscar in the garbage can talks to Big Bird—what kind of idiocy is that? We all know that interesting and even educational ideas are often "irrelevant." Of course, we have to tolerate a certain degree of relevance, but let's acknowledge that it's often boring.

VII

We won't be reaching our students if we insist on emphasizing sequential learning either. A while back Piaget was resurrected and reintroduced into the curriculum. Few understand what he's saying but he is a world-renowned research psychologist. Though his work is fascinating, it has, in my judgment, little value for understanding the way children learn (very few of my colleagues agree with me on this matter).

Generally, significant learning does not take place sequentially, as has been suggested by Piaget. People learn things in random order as suits them best individually, and at varying speeds. How else can we account for the fact that language is not absorbed in a sequential way? Children under five can often learn several languages far easier than adults can. It appears terribly important to encourage young children to learn abstract, complicated concepts early in life, even before the age of five. Although tailoring the classroom to suit individual needs is admittedly difficult, we can start to move in the direction of providing for our slower and faster students who are not average in any sense of the word.

VIII

Advice such as "Pay attention . . ." can be of benefit only if it is seen as a goal, and not something that is immediately practicable. Let me illustrate.

I survived my public school career by daydreaming. A teacher once said to me that she was impressed by what I said in a speech about daydreaming as well as the difficulty of following advice. This is what subsequently happened. In the middle of a lecture in astronomy she suddenly saw this kid who was daydreaming. She remembered what I had said about not intruding because the daydream might be more important than anything she had to contribute. And as soon as she remembered, she began to stutter and didn't know what to say or do and forgot her lesson. The students began to laugh, and finally she couldn't stand it anymore. So she said to the student, "Stop daydreaming!" She felt marvelous after that and continued her lesson.

This teacher learned something by not being able to follow

advice. She learned that the problem was not so much that the child was daydreaming but that she couldn't stand it! Don't advise your students to pay attention with the expectation that they can easily comply.

If you have students who act up in class, don't tell them to behave because they won't listen to that. They might do the opposite. Instead, try this—take them aside and say, "Look. It's hard for you to sit still in class. So tomorrow why don't you get up and sharpen your pencil often, pass notes, and don't pay any attention to me?" Give them permission for their distractibility. (Much more often than not the other children in the classroom will understand what you are doing.)

They may respond, "What do you think I am? Don't you think I can behave if I want to once in a while?" Make them aware at the same time of the impact they are having on other students. By giving permission, they won't need to be so misbehaved, although this certainly isn't a cure-all and for some it won't work at all. Some scenes are inevitable with students who really can't help acting up occasionally.

IX

Listen to the suggestions or complaints of your students who have handicaps and don't be afraid to admit that the difficulty may be at least partly your fault. Some students may be typically argumentative or dissatisfied, but some of their thoughts are bound to be justified, albeit they may be communicated in an irritating manner.

If special attention and methods are required, it may be helpful to explain to the rest of the class your motivation. All pupils should understand that their taunts and jokes hurt the handicapped, but that their support and friendship would be gladly welcomed. This is generally made easier by segregating the handicapped as little as necessary, and by explaining why periodic absences from class to see the psychologist or special education teacher are required.

Students can be encouraged to modify the rules of their games somewhat so the handicapped can participate—i.e., they may be able to be the batter or kicker and have someone else run the bases for them. Your own enthusiastic and cooperative spirit will be likely to be absorbed by the students.

X

A minimum of academic skills is, it is hoped, possible for most students who have handicaps. Probably a sixth-grade level in reading and arithmetic is sufficient for the ordinary requirements of daily living, such as reading an evening paper, making change, filling out application forms, handling a checking account. If at all possible, any child should be helped to achieve this level of functioning.

It may be known to the reader that I am among a minority of professionals who have not been happy about the current fad of lumping all the educationally handicapped into a category of "learning disabled." Apart from the fact that some brain-injured youth do not have learning disabilities, I am convinced that the learning problems of the mentally retarded, emotionally disturbed, the so-called disadvantaged, and the neurologically impaired differ from each other and often require quite different remediation procedures.

This is an argument, however, that will not be settled in my time. Suffice it to say that the meaning of "psychological time," as that concept relates to classwork and manifest boredom, has never been adequately explored. It would be interesting to know why some children will stand at a pinball machine for hours when they seem to be hyperactive in the classroom; or why they will practice football into the darkness, or why a pool hall is less boring than a classroom. Perhaps if this knowledge becomes available, it might be possible to teach persistence and involvement directly instead of hoping that these attitudes are "caught" as the child moves through the grades. It is also becoming increasingly clear that there are sound techniques for teaching basic skills to youth with learning disabilities. For example, it is exciting to observe how much learning can take place in the context of games, hobbies, and crafts. Individualizing instruction is the key to sound educational management.

We had better concern ourselves with the psychological dimensions of people having trouble learning. We had better understand that a lot of our young people may be hyperactive, they may have short attention spans, and they may not be able to handle anything that's not concrete. They may not be able to deal with anything that isn't relevant, but I say it is curious that the way we have described the learning disabled is the same way we have described the blacks, the Puerto Ricans, the disadvantaged, and the emotionally disturbed.

XI

If I were to make any generalization about youth with learning problems, I would refer to their lack of self-awareness, especially with reference to their impact on others. Part of the explanation for this is their lack of experience owing to isolation, but another aspect seems to be related to their inability to absorb abstract ideas easily. We must, therefore, devise training methods that compensate for this deficit. Thus, direct instruction guidance, learning by doing, and the like, seem to be indicated, rather than expecting the youth to be able to anticipate behavior or to profit from previous related experience. Counseling groups are often beneficial in this area. (Individual psychotherapeutic sessions, which focus on insight or intellectualization, are seldom helpful.)

Helping youth to make lighthearted admissions of deficits

helps to make them and others comfortable with their limitations—"Let me watch you play, baseball just isn't my bag," or "Let me unload the equipment rather than take notes. My writing is like a foreign language!"

Youth are much more likely to respond favorably to peers than to their parents when told such things as the following: "You are repeating yourself." "Jean, this is a beautiful dress. It looks good on you." "You talk too loudly." "Hey, don't you have any manners?"

XII

If I walk into an institution or a school or classroom for people with handicaps, and a child comes to me and says, "Do you love me?" I would say, "No." It's not good for them to feel that everybody loves them, because not everyone does. So many young children are hugging and kissing everybody and we are so nice in saying, "Oh, yes, we love you." This is not a good idea. We can render them unsocializable and encourage inappropriate behavior by being too nice and not really being honest with them.

XIII

Sometimes we try to explain weird behavior by giving it a name—such as perseveration, which means you repeat yourself over and over again. It's really called being a pain in the neck. Take the kid in the classroom who is saying, "Did I do all right? Did I do good? Did I do all right?"

The teacher says to herself silently, "I wish this kid would leave me alone; he's driving me crazy." But to the child, the teacher's saying, "Yes, honey, you're doing all right. You're doing good work." What is this teacher doing? Simply reinforcing inappropriate behavior. What should this teacher (and the parents) do? They should say, "Bunny (or whatever the name happens to be), listen. Every time you ask for praise, I'm not going to give it to you. Even if you deserve it, because you ask for praise a lot. I don't enjoy it, and the other kids don't appreciate it." The student may not like what you say and may go home with the complaint "The teacher doesn't like me anymore," but it's a small price to pay for the inappropriate behavior being extinguished in a few weeks' time.

XIV

I once taught a high school class with youngsters who had learning disabilities. I thought to myself, "I am such an interesting teacher. I should be able to do the job that no other teacher has been able to do. And besides, what could be more stimulating than psychology? We'll talk about dreams and fantasies, jokes and their meaning and relation to the unconscious. We'll talk about hypnosis and so many exciting things." I suspect every teacher has delusions such as these at some time or another.

In the front of my class sat a big 6-foot-3 basketball player who said to me, "Doc, nobody teaches in this class without my consent."

I looked at him and said, "Well, may I have your consent?" Nobody had ever responded to him in this way! It was always, "What do you mean I need your consent? Go down to the principal!"

And he replied in answer to my question, "Sure, Doc."

As I started to talk to the class, he began to snore audibly. I asked, "Why aren't you letting me teach this class?"

"Oh, I don't know. I'm tired. I had a hard day. Besides, I changed my mind."

And I said, "Don, how would you like me to analyze you?"

He replied, "Okay. But on one condition—providing that I can analyze you afterwards."

I said okay. "Don, the problem with you is that you feel so insecure and so unsure of your masculinity that you need to demonstrate it all the time."

"Hey, Doc. Come on, let's go to the bathroom and I'll show you what's masculine about me."

"That's not what I was talking about. I'm not interested in the size of your penis."

He became very interested in what I had to say and finally he said to me, "Now I'm going to tell you a thing or two." Don, who was at a third-grade reading and arithmetic level in high school, said, "You know, I represent the unconscious of all the young people in this school who are not achieving and not learning. We are the lost generation and I want to tell you something—we're going to make as much trouble as possible, because you have created so many of our problems!" I thought I had it made with him and the class and could do the most exciting things!

The next day the students wouldn't let me teach. They were throwing spitballs and shouting as I desperately tried to teach, and finally I said, "I give up like everybody else."

I didn't say to them, "You're no good." I said, "I'm no good." After all, I'm the teacher. Why do I have to be so proud? Why do I say to kids, "Pay attention" or "Shut up" or "Go to the principal"? Why can't I communicate with them by saying, "I'm sorry that I'm boring you" or "I'm sorry that I can't communicate. I should be able to communicate but I'm not able to"? I may have to send a kid to the office, but I say, "Look, I'm sorry I have to do this but I have to teach the other students. I feel badly that we can't get along." I don't have to be overwhelmed with guilt or blame myself so fully it disorganizes me. I know that somehow if I had a smaller class and if I had the time and if there were other circumstances, I would have been able to do something. Eventually my students and I came to an understanding for classroom procedure and cooperation, but not until I realized that many of the students equated education with submission.

XV

Those of you who are teachers, pay only limited attention to what I'm saying unless you have tenure. And while I'm at it: If you're doing something creative in your classroom that works, don't tell anybody! Keep it to yourself, because as soon as "they" discover that you're doing something creative, somebody will tell you that you're not following the curriculum.

The same censorship is likely to apply if a teacher or school tries to teach something about sex. I'm not a big advocate of sex education in the schools, because it belongs mainly in the home. I'm not saying that a certain amount of sex education should not be in the schools, for the handicapped or otherwise. There are actually schools in this country where the chapter on human reproduction has been torn from the biology textbooks. You can't teach history and about Queen Victoria without talking about her sex attitudes. (But it's done all the time.) You can't teach about physiology without talking about human reproduction, nor is health complete without discussing venereal disease and its prevention.

We studied two hundred major curricula in health in which mention was made of venereal disease. They told how you get it and what you do when you got it, but there wasn't one single reference to prevention other than abstinence. There wasn't a single statement about the use of the condom, which is a good method of prevention. That's immaturity and censorship in the schools. We have allowed small groups of right-wing elements to dominate what should and should not be in schools, what books belong in the library, and so on. Some think that sex education is a communist plot (don't laugh). They know that there are enough ignorant people in this country who will believe this, and they know they can use it as subterfuge to acquire power. What's more, there are still people who think that knowledge about sex will stimulate inappropriate behavior. All the studies we have reviewed reveal the opposite. Ignorance is not bliss.

XVI

Of course, there is not one solution suitable for everybody or for all problems in our schools. I am disturbed by people who claim, "Everybody should be integrated," or whatever. Yet, not everyone can tolerate it: For some it is an enormously unhelpful situation. I do favor integration whenever possible, and it's usually more possible than is thought to be the case.

Conclusion

Recently I was invited to tour an institution for the mentally retarded. Along the way a young man about twenty-two years old intruded upon our company and said to me, "Hey, you! What's your name?" I didn't say anything. I ignored him and continued on my way. My hosts tried to shoo him away, but he was not shoo-awayable, and he intruded again. He looked at me and said, "Hey, you! Are you married?" Again I didn't respond, and, of course, my guides were very upset because they thought they had invited an expert on mental retardation, and he wasn't even nice to the mentally retarded. They tried to shoo him away once more, but still he was not shoo-awayable. "Hey, you!" he shouted at me. "I want to know your name." Then I looked at him and I said, "Sir, I don't know who you are, and I don't have to talk to you." He regarded me for a moment and said, "Hmm, you have a point. I'm sorry to approach you in this way but I was curious to find out who you were, and I wanted to talk to you." It was one of my finest teaching moments because we sat down and for twenty minutes had an intelligent conversation. The people in the institution were astonished because until that time they had not realized that this young man was not mentally retarded but was, indeed, learning disabled.

I didn't need any fancy psychological examination. I didn't need any medical studies, or anything except the opportunity to talk to him in a manner that suggested I respected him. The way we treat people is the way they are going to respond to us!

21

A Nonreading Approach to Reading

*Signs** is a response to the failure of traditional curricula to teach fundamental reading skills to students. Although regular methods work well for those who are motivated and have no learning problems, it is essential to provide for those who *are* blocked. This is one possible approach in a field that needs many approaches to satisfy individual problems.

Signs is a series of four booklets, one a teacher's guide; the other three contain photographs of signs and people interacting in different situations. In some photographs there is a central theme and in others the focus may be several simultaneous happenings. They stimulate the imagination and introduce abstract ideas and unfamiliar environments which provide many

* *Signs* is available from New Readers Press, Box 131, Syracuse, N.Y. 13210. A filmstrip version is available from Educational Activities, Box 392, Freeport, N.Y. 11520.

students with a better chance to learn later on. Photographs are chosen for their ability to excite and arouse curiosity.

The *Signs* approach to teaching reading is based on a series of assumptions concerning how children learn to read. The first is that every child already can read somewhat before the formal learning process begins. Such terms as pizza, Howard Johnson, rest room, and exit are familiar simply in day-to-day living. The words themselves differ according to the culture and environment, but stimulation from the media, billboards, stores, and other sources puts the youth in touch with some words that are easily memorized.

The books in the *Signs* series are neither texts nor basal readers. They are designed to interest poor readers or nonreading adults and children in words and experiences before formal reading instruction or after formal attempts have been unsuccessful. There is no particular sequence involved in using *Signs*, since limiting initial learning experiences to routine and familiar concepts may deaden motivation and performance.

As a student views a photograph, the instructor is requested not to teach reading at all. The purpose is to stimulate discussion and interest. If some students recognize the words and signs, it is simply accepted without making the mistake of saying "Yes, that says grocery. What other words start with the letter 'G'?"

Everyone who looks at a photograph will see things in a slightly different way and interpret them accordingly. There are no right or wrong answers: Everyone can tell what he sees in a photograph, what it reminds him of. The prospect of giving correct responses bolsters self-confidence and gradually builds the ability to offer one's contribution in other areas as well. Persons who are blocked in reading, have a disability, and/or are alienated by past learning experiences can begin to open up. Photographs can also give students who enjoy reading a respite from regular class work and provide a basis for sharing knowledge and experiences among students.

Students can take an active interest and role in using *Signs*. Encourage them to make up their own dialogues and to invent stories growing out of the photograph. A student could prepare a tape for presentation or you could transcribe spoken words if no tape recorders are handy.

Inventive games and activities spring from the photographs. For example, play a tape or read a monologue, and have the students select the one of several photographs that corresponds to it. Even if you have a tape recorder available, you might want to begin the initial presentation in person, since some students are more captivated by a live narrator.

Encourage your students to imagine what went on before and after the photographs were taken.

Let two or more students assume the roles of the people and have a conversation based on the photographs.

Students who own or have access to cameras can be encouraged to take their own photographs.

As these valuable verbal skills increase and you have been as inventive as you please, you will want to turn your attention to the next phase of language development, reading and writing. Words will make a lot more sense once your students understand how vividly they represent real-life situations, people, friends, things, everything, even themselves. The most appropriate point of departure is the class work and experiences you have already done orally. Students are especially familiar with and interested in their own work.

The idea is to prepare written scripts of the students' oral work. First, have the students tape their responses and role plays if they have not already done so, and transcribe the tapes. Or simply transcribe the students' words as they speak. The connection is then complete: students participate in a natural sequence of language development. Ultimately, students will be reading their own words (and peers'), which maintains a high level of interest. Beginning readers often read the same or similar material over and over again and become bored with the monotony.

Finally, the same photographs can be used effectively with both children and adults. The responses and level of interest may differ significantly, but nearly everyone enjoys looking at and discussing photographs: Prekindergarten or first grade, young people who have already learned to hate to read or whose intellectual or perceptual abilities are limited (learning disabled and some brain injured), or adults who never learned to read adequately.

Signs is also useful for non-English-speaking children and adults who are new to America or who live outside the mainstream of society. American life and culture are aptly represented, since the contents vary and the words range from the simple to the complex.

We present this approach as one we believe is effective in communicating with readers. There are few routines or rules, necessary guidelines or procedures, which would turn off unstructured students. Once teachers understand the concept of *Signs*, they can adapt it to any given situation, culture, and language, using photographs of local attractions and people as the basis for discussions. Although we acknowledge that there are other acceptable methods for motivating and educating, this approach is often more effective than remediation with its attentive pressure and anxiety. It is in a sense preremedial. Once the students regain confidence they can then be given formal reading instruction.

22

Alternative Approaches for Teaching Mathematics

by Ronald S. Horowitz

This chapter is divided into three general sections: Section I is primarily for teachers of students who possess very limited arithmetic skills. As a consequence games and related activities are recommended for motivational reasons. Section II contains important and basic mathematical operations which are recommended for those who elect to learn about them. For students who memorize techniques, but are unable to advance beyond an elementary level, Section III includes practical applications which are directly related to social acceptance. This material originally appeared, in somewhat different form, in *Academic Therapy*, Vol. VI, 1, Fall 1970, pp. 17–35.

Section I

Failure to acquire basic mathematical skills is often due to a lack of readiness, ineffectual teaching, or a combination of both. Rote memorization contributes to a weak foundation, and a cycle of failure evolves into a block for all mathematics. Teachers feel guilty when they do not follow the "guidelines" of a standardized curriculum, and students respond to questions as a quest for success in peer competitiveness, irrespective of correct solutions. Even an appropriate response is not a clear indicator of comprehension. In *How Children Fail*, John Holt stated:

> We must not fool ourselves, as for years I fooled myself into thinking that guiding children to answer by carefully chosen leading questions in any respect is different from just telling them the answer in the first place. Children who have been led up to answers by teacher's questions are later helpless unless they can remember the questions or ask themselves similar questions, and this is exactly what they can't do. The only answer that really sticks in a child's mind is the answer that he asked or might ask himself.[*]

Teachers and parents have been subjected to a barrage of cures. Traditional curriculum guides and recipe-lesson-plans have been supplanted by the "new math," and old wooden blocks have been renamed "rods." Rather than giving new answers, many of these approaches are based on memorization and manipulation. *Alternative* methods described in this article are based on the following assumptions:

Students with a psychological block to mathematics need a personal relationship of trust. Informal methods which

[*] John Holt, *How Children Fail* (New York: Pitman Publishing Corp., 1964, p. 119).

are thoughtfully monitored are invariably more useful than an overemphasis on basic skills.

Popular games, hobbies, and related activities can be used as a *basis* for instruction (most popular games have survived because they are more interesting and pertinent than "innovative" curriculum games).

A guide does not have to be used as a "package," but rather can become an outline from which many alternatives are selected for experimentation.

Memorization alone may hinder a student's ability to apply factual information.

Teachers are often more handicapped than students. Instruction should not be initiated until the student is ready to begin.

Substantive learning can occur within a framework of games, hobbies, crafts, and other self-stimulating media. Games provide a high motivational environment which can be used to develop a student's ability to cope with stress and complexity. Strategies in some games, puzzles, and crafts often suggest causal relationships corresponding to operations in formal mathematics. Experience has demonstrated that it is difficult to judge which games children can play—it should not be assumed that a "poor" mathematics student cannot learn complicated games.

Short attention span, distractibility, and lack of interest are sometimes cited as reasons why some children are not learning. These symptoms are often the result of boredom. It is fascinating to observe "highly distractible" children spending hours playing with pinball machines, cards, dice, and other games.

The following criteria are considered essential to an adequate learning environment:

Providing initial success for the student in the program

of study by creating an environment that allows opportunities for questioning and decision-making.

Maintaining a high-interest environment.

Determining areas of inadequacy: poor understanding of vocabulary and concepts as well as language problems.

Noting inconsistencies in the student's thinking ability. For example, the student who plays dominoes and cribbage but has not learned to multiply and divide fractions.

Decreasing the levels of anxiety related to mathematical instruction.

Maintaining continuity between lessons.

Removing classroom formality is critical to innovation.* The relationship between teacher and student must take place in a relaxed atmosphere where basic mathematical concepts are incidentally introduced. If students have encountered negative experiences in mathematics classrooms, applications of vocabulary meaning, discriminations, relationships, and so on can be observed more realistically in an open environment.

Games provide opportunities for increased socialization, which is vital to all students. A thorough knowledge of the rules and concepts involved in indoor and outdoor games and activities is invaluable to all children.

Following is a suggested procedure for using games as a basis for introducing mathematics:

Ask the student to select items from the following List A (Stimulation Media) that he or she knows how to play and would be willing to play, or would enjoy being taught.

Explain that in exchange for playing with these games,

* See *The Learning Community, The Language of an Alternative* for a description of a significant alternative model within public education which has been designed for a cross-section of students, and has eliminated dependence on classes. Copies are available from *The Learning Community*, Princeton Regional Schools, Princeton, N.J. 08540.

puzzles, crafts, etc., others will be selected that are also valuable and interesting.

During play, observe inaccurate and inconsistent applications of vocabulary meanings, relationships, discriminations, etc., in List B (Vocabulary Development).

Teach games that will most clearly meet apparent conceptual difficulties and insure opportunities to transfer concepts into new situations.

For example, a student might select checkers as one of the games he is willing to play. The teacher then selects items from List B that can be appropriately diagnosed and taught while playing checkers: (1) from Discriminations—up and down, front and back, diagonal and across, in front of and behind; (2) from Relationships—color of objects, number of objects, and comparing unequal sets; (3) from Abilities—recognize number of elements in a group without counting.

While playing a game, a therapist can observe problematic discriminations, vocabulary meanings, and abilities. To continue with the example of the game of checkers, the therapist finds that the student understands all objectives except the relationship between *diagonal and across,* and decides to teach Monopoly and chess (from List A) in order to present the required discriminations and relationships. A teacher can be a catalyst to the thinking process by providing numerous alternatives for succeeding.

Popular outdoor games direct the motion of the body into the learning experience. Every child who participates in football or kickball makes use of basic mathematical discriminations and relationships. Arithmetical skills are applied in scoring football, bowling, and other games.

An effective curriculum based on games is not *only* game playing. Initially, the teacher's role is to find *any* game that the student enjoys playing. If many options are offered, most

LIST A: STIMULATION MEDIA

GAMES (G)

1. Chess
2. Draughts
3. Backgammon
4. Dice games
5. Checkers
6. Whist
7. Bridge
8. Cinch
9. Pinochle
10. Sixty-six
11. Hearts
12. Rummy
13. Casino
14. Solitaire
15. Cribbage
16. Poker
17. Bowling
18. Mah-Jongg
19. W'ff 'n Proof
20. On-sets
21. Monopoly
22. Yahtze
23. Parcheesi
24. Buzz
25. Simon Says
26. Shuffleboard
27. Follow the Dots
28. Lotto
29. Bingo
30. Hopscotch
31. Pencil games
32. Darts
33. Twenty-one
34. Pick-up Sticks
35. Baseball
36. Kickball
37. Dodgeball
38. Tennis
39. Badminton
40. Volleyball
41. Tetherball
42. Soccer
43. Field hockey
44. Basketball
45. Golf
46. Croquet
47. Relay games
48. Jumping games
49. Track events
50. Spud
51. Ice skating
52. Swimming
53. Fishing
54. Hunting

ACTIVITIES AND SKILLS (A)

1. Abacus
2. Map making
3. Graphing
4. Mixing chemical solutions
5. Designing house plans
6. Designing games
7. Operating cash registers
8. Puzzles and "fitting toys"
9. Stocks (actual or simulated manipulation)
10. Slide rule

LIST A (continued)
ACTIVITIES AND SKILLS (A)
(continued)

11. Pedometer
12. Cooking (measuring cups)
13. Totaling and estimating
14. Restaurant tips

HOBBIES (H)

1. Model construction
2. Stamp collecting

3. Erector sets
4. Coin collecting
5. Photography
6. Sports (scoring, record keeping)
7. Number painting
8. Collecting historical data
9. Collecting match covers, baseball cards, etc.

LIST B: VOCABULARY DEVELOPMENT

VOCABULARY MEANINGS (V)

1. same
2. plus
3. none
4. many
5. whole
6. part
7. minus
8. next
9. beneath
10. round
11. group
12. nickel
13. subtract
14. quarter
15. one-half
16. set
17. inch
18. feet
19. yard
20. union
21. corner

22. meter
23. centimeter
24. dozen
25. allowance
26. fare
27. one-fourth
28. high
29. wide
30. a.m. and p.m.
31. dollar
32. per
33. cash
34. C.O.D.
35. down payment
36. installment
37. annual
38. semiannual
39. depth
40. quarterly
41. tax
42. collection

LIST B (continued)
VOCABULARY   MEANINGS
  (V)
(continued)

43. greater than
44. less than
45. digit
46. exact
47. zero
48. add
49. circular
50. dime
51. buck
52. multiply
53. divide

DISCRIMINATIONS

1. up, down
2. in, out
3. on, off
4. big, little
5. front, back
6. right, left
7. slow, fast
8. thick, thin
9. most, least
10. light, heavy
11. first, last
12. above, below
13. short, long
14. forward, backward
15. diagonal, across
16. all, none
17. empty, full
18. narrow, wide
19. more, less
20. few, many

21. quickly, slowly
22. less than, more than
23. large, small
24. top, bottom
25. in front of, behind
26. same, different
27. expensive, cheap
28. uptown, downtown
29. higher, lower

RELATIONSHIPS (R)

1. color of objects
2. number of objects
3. shape of objects
4. conserving numbers
5. conserving substance
6. comparing unequal sets
7. ordering size of objects
8. relating sets of subsets
9. "to" and "after" (relating to time)
10. addition and multiplication
11. subtraction and division
12. hour and minute
13. second and minute
14. ounce and pound
15. inch to foot
16. pint to quart
17. nickel to dime

ABILITIES (A)

1. add and subtract with objects
2. tell time
3. make change
4. count by rote
5. read number symbols

LIST B (continued)
ABILITIES (A)
(continued)

6. understanding money values
7. use ruler for measuring
8. comprehend fractional concepts
9. add in columns
10. add two-place numbers

11. subtract
12. identify money using decimal rotation
13. totaling and estimating restaurant bills
14. match time with daily activities
15. recognize number of elements in a group without counting

students will attempt new games if they are allowed stipulated periods when they can play games of their choice.

Some students are intrigued by games where chance rather than skill determines the outcome. Even games with a high chance component, such as dice and some card games, contain many developmental objectives which can be observed (see Lists A and B). Of course, movement toward games of skill is desirable.

A chart which includes games and developmental objectives follows.

Section II

The approach in this section relies on the student's past mathematical knowledge, his personal experiences, and concrete objects as a basis for understanding concepts. Thus, it frees the teacher from presenting abstractions and allows him or her to think and teach as freely and realistically in mathematics as he or she would in other subjects.

Education rarely takes place when a teacher is "ahead of" or "too slow" for the student. This situation occurs frequently with compulsive use of traditional lectures, kits, guides, and the like, which are geared to the "average" student. Physical objects, such as blocks, rods, and games, are useful. The remedial

STIMULATION-OBJECTIVE CHART

STIMULATION PREFERRED (Games selected by student)	DEVELOPMENT OBJECTIVES (To be observed by tutor while playing)	APPARENT DEVELOPMENT REQUIRED (Vocabulary)	STIMULATION Suggested and Taught
G5 Checkers	D1 up, down D5 front, back D15 diagonal, across D25 in front of, behind R1 color of objects R2 number of objects R6 comparing unequal sets A15 recognize number of elements in a group without counting	D15 diagonal, across V7 minus	G1 Chess G21 Monopoly A1 add and subtract with objects
G21 Monopoly	V10 round V33 cash V35 down payment V36 installment V41 tax	A3 make change A6 understand money values	G29 Bingo A13 totaling and estimating restaurant bills

therapist, however, must consider each individual's experiences and levels of understanding.

It is possible to sustain the attention of virtually any student for five or possibly ten minutes. During this time, concepts are presented and the student is encouraged to give related examples from his own experience, from physical objects, and from past mathematical knowledge, to explain or manipulate the concepts.

Following are suggestions for presenting a "formal" lesson:

> After assessing the child's ability from diagnostic impressions, the teacher gives a five-minute lesson and one or two appropriate examples which illustrate the mathematical ideas or concepts. It is important to avoid explanations or examples which are purely manipulative.
>
> The teacher elicits from the student three or more examples which are similar to the ones presented.
>
> Key questions are asked that will induce the students to respond creatively: Can you show me _____? Can you think of _____? What things at home are shaped like _____? Can the concept be illustrated by using objects in the classroom, such as blocks, rods, chairs?
>
> For the remainder of the lesson, the child is asked to demonstrate the property, idea, or concept presented. When the child offers personal examples, he or she will be able to generalize from them and compare them to the principles being explained in the lesson. This process should not be hurried. Rather than criticize the inappropriate examples, try to understand the *reasoning* which produced them.

An illustrated lesson follows:

The topic to be discussed today is the addition of fractions. I will give an example of two fractions being added:

Numerically $\frac{1}{4} + \frac{3}{4} = ?$

Example:

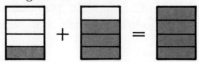

A concrete answer: $\frac{1}{4}$ of a glass of milk plus $\frac{3}{4}$ of a glass of milk is equal to 1 whole glass of milk, so that numerically $\frac{1}{4} + \frac{3}{4} = 1$.

Another Example:
(Pizza Pies)

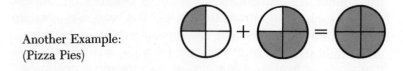

Again, $\frac{1}{4}$ of a pizza added to $\frac{3}{4}$ of a pizza is the same as 1 whole pizza; this is another example which demonstrates that $\frac{1}{4} + \frac{3}{4} = \frac{4}{4}$ or 1.

Homework question: Continue to create four more examples that will clearly demonstrate that $\frac{1}{4} + \frac{3}{4} = 1$.

The teacher might be able to elicit a few examples such as the following:

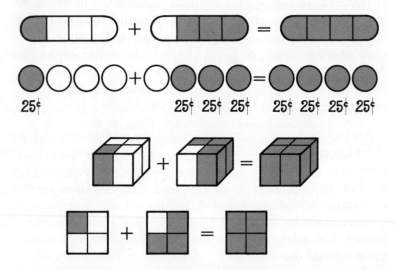

The above homework examples reveal that the student has a clear notion of why $\frac{1}{4} + \frac{3}{4} = 1$. Some students have difficulty thinking of *any* examples. "Fractional" pies, blocks, or physical objects can help elicit examples.

The following curriculum topics include addition, subtraction, multiplication, division, fractions, and decimals. Each of the topics described below can be used as a basis for a series of five-minute lessons. Suggestions are included to facilitate introducing each topic. Unless students can cite examples to demonstrate the concepts, it should not be assumed that they understand them.

When a student cannot comprehend a particular concept or proceed beyond a given level, refer to the approach in Section I to search for misunderstood or inadequate vocabulary, discriminations, and relationships.

ADDITION: *Adding* and also *plus* means "putting together," whether it be chairs, people, blocks, whole numbers, fractions, or decimals. In the process of addition, the order in which the sets of objects or numbers are placed together or added is not critical. That is, five chairs plus one chair is the same as one chair plus five chairs, or $1 + 5 = 5 + 1$. In *any* examples that demonstrate addition, this condition will always be true. Some important vocabulary meanings are *plus, sum, total, more than,* and *greater than.*

SUBTRACTION: Subtraction is the act of "taking away." A set of four books can be "taken away," "separated," or subtracted from a set of seven books. The result will always represent the number of objects left. It is also possible to reverse any subtraction with a corresponding addition of the same quantity.

In subtraction, the order of operation is *not* reversible. In other words, $5 - 2 \neq 2 - 5$, or we can't take \$5.00 away from \$2.00 and arrive at the same conclusion as when we take \$2.00 away from \$5.00. The possibility of error in expressing a subtraction problem is therefore greater than in addition. Vocabulary distinctions include *less than, subtracted from,* and *minus.*

MULTIPLICATION: Since multiplication is a series of additions, a firm knowledge of addition must precede. Any multiplication problem can be expressed as an addition problem, for example, $3 \times 4 = 4 + 4 + 4$. Comprehending words like *product, times, multiplier,* etc., is essential.

DIVISION: Division can be viewed as a series of subtractions. $6 \div 2 = ?$ The question asks how many sets of 2 there are in 6. The answer represents how many sets of 2 there are in 6, namely 3. Since $8 \div 2 \neq 2 \div 8$, there must be literal translation of the division sign. For example, there are two sets of four objects in eight objects, but there are not two sets of eight objects in four objects.

FRACTIONS: *Most* students encounter difficulty with fractional operations. Students who understand the most simple fractions can usually draw pictures to represent the respective concept. Their understanding should not be limited to the abstract.

When any fraction is presented, a student should be taken to a point where he can easily demonstrate three or four examples which illustrate fractional portions.

DECIMALS: Decimals are related to fractional concepts. Many students are familiar with baseball averages or test grading systems. Decimals provide an alternative method for working with fractions.

Section III

Some students experience little difficulty memorizing new rules but may be unable to interpret them. They may be able to add and subtract numbers successfully but not be able to count their change when purchasing an item. In such cases, the therapist can organize and classify similar experiences. It is often assumed that when mathematical topics are useful—for example, making change or counting money—they are easier to learn. Often schools interrupt learning in this regard by enforcing only normative grade-level pressures.

The table "Topics and Activities" that follows illustrates how popular and commercial games (see "Materials and Sources" list for names of manufacturers), hobbies, skills, activities, etc., can be related to basic mathematical topics. There relationships can be enhanced and the model expanded. Many applications can be supplemented by the procedure developed in Section I and the more formalized structures given in Section II.

The approaches for teaching mathematics to handicapped students presented in this chapter emphasize the use of games and other high-motivational materials, and while far from being comprehensive, are found to be particularly appealing for those who have had negative experiences with mathematics. In the final analysis, the pupil-teacher relationship is a primary determinant of success or failure, and it is in the spirit of the methods suggested that this relationship can be positively accentuated.

TOPICS AND ACTIVITIES

TOPIC	ACTIVITY	RELATED GAMES, HOBBIES, SKILLS, ETC.	COMMERCIAL GAMES
Price of Articles	Talking about prices of clothes, sports equipment, cars, and other items of interest; discussing what a fixed amount of money would purchase. Discussing simple tax problems, such as sales tax.	Operating cash registers and business machines Stocks (simulated or actual manipulation) Coin collecting Bingo (for prizes) Poker and other card games (for money or chips)	Catalogs Newspapers Magazines Billboards Advertisement
Weights and Measurements	Discussing ounces, quarts, pints, gallons, and their relationships. Determining gas costs for a trip about the area. Using scales to weigh different objects and discussing relationship between liquid and solid weights. Also, talking about costs per lb. and ton of different products, ordering materials by mail (parcel post) to determine cost of postage per fixed weight.	Cooking Baking Mixing chemical solutions Photography (processing) Track events	Pi-O Math Labs Liquid Measure Set Liter Measure Meter Sticks Board Foot Cubic Foot Yardsticks Giant Ruler

Money	Relating the values of pennies, nickels, dimes, quarters, and dollars and "making change."	Monopoly Card games (for money or chips) Operating cash registers and business machines Coin collecting	
Scoring	Learning how to keep score in athletic events and individual games.	Bridge Football Pinochle Basketball Hearts Golf Rummy Bowling Poker Dice games Twenty-one Whist Designing games	
Time	Telling time and discussing relationship between seconds, minutes, hours, days, and time zones. Distinguishing between a.m., p.m. and calendar awareness, relationship recurrence of important holidays.	All games where specific time periods can be incorporated Relay games Mixing chemical solutions (and observing reaction times) Cooking and baking	Pendulum Clock Kit See-Through Alarm Clock Racemaster Stopwatch Sequential Calendar

TOPICS AND ACTIVITIES (continued)

TOPIC	ACTIVITY	RELATED GAMES, HOBBIES, SKILLS, ETC.	COMMERCIAL GAMES
		Photography (shutter speeds)	Time and Time Telling (text)
		Chess (using tournament clocks)	Build-a-Clock
		Horoscope	
Large Numbers	Discussing city, country, and minority-group populations, as well as significant economic statistics (millions, billions, etc.).	Basketball	Calculator
		Running (five-hundred)	Digi-Comp
		Paper and pencil games	Structural Arithmetic Kits
		Operating business machines	
		Reading meters	
Comparing Speeds	Comparing the relative speeds (miles/hour, feet/second, etc.) of birds, cars, airplanes, etc.	Track and field events	Magnetic Globe Game
		Swimming	
		Skating	
Geometric Shapes	Distinguishing between rectangles, squares, circles, triangles, and other common distinctions.	Chess	Shape-Sorting Box
		Mah-Jongg	300 Box
		Monopoly	Jigsaw Cone
		Fitting toys and puzzles	Rubber Fit-in Puzzles
		Model construction	

		Hopscotch	Wood Palm Puzzles
		Dominoes	Form Perception Box
		Dice	Giant Template Set
		Cards	Geometric Form Cards
			Shape Puzzles
			Shape Matching Series
Measuring	Develop practice problems which involve finding height, length, width, perimeter, area of rooms, objects, etc. Requires actual measurement. On maps, measuring distance between cities, reading scale of the map, plotting trips, etc.	Map-making, map-reading	Pedometer
		Pedometer	Measure-Up (text)
		Paper and pencil games (involving measurement)	Pi-Math Labs
		Pin tail on donkey	Math Projects:
		Construction tasks	Map Making
		Fitting toys and puzzles	Color Dominoes
		Model construction	Counting Box & Spindles
		Shuffleboard	Count-A-Line
		Designing house plans	
		Golf	
		Monopoly	

REFERENCES

These publications were consulted in preparing this chapter, and provide teachers with a good foundation for alternative approaches for teaching mathematics.

Bruner, J. S. *The Process of Education*, Cambridge, Mass.: Harvard University Press, 1960.

Featherstone, Joseph. "How Children Learn," *The New Republic*, September 2, 1967.

Goals for School Mathematics, Report of the Cambridge Conference on School Mathematics. Boston, Mass.: Houghton Mifflin Company, 1963.

Holt, John. *How Children Fail*. New York, N.Y.: Pitman Publishing Corp., Inc., 1964.

Kaplan, Jerome D. "Mathematical Objectives," unpublished. New York, N.Y.: Institute for Developmental Studies, School of Education, New York University, 1966.

Neill, A. S. *Summerhill: A Radical Approach to Child Rearing*. New York, N.Y.: Hart Publishing Company, 1960.

Paschal, Bill J. "A Concerned Teacher Makes the Difference," *The Arithmetic Teacher*, XIII (March 1966), 203–205.

Information about Developments Pertaining to the Mathematics Curriculum:

Ausubel, David P. *The Psychology of Meaningful Verbal Learning*. New York, N.Y.: Grune & Stratton, Inc., 1963.

Beilin, Harry, and Lassar G. Gotkin. "Psychological Issues in the Development of Mathematics Curricula for Socially Disadvantaged Children," unpublished. New York, N.Y.: Institute for Developmental Studies, Brooklyn College, 1964.

Berkeley, Edmund C. *A Guide to Mathematics for the Intelligent Non-mathematician*. New York, N.Y.: Simon & Schuster, Inc., 1966.

Piaget, Jean. *The Child's Conception of Number*. New York, N.Y.: W. W. Norton & Company, Inc., 1965.

Reed, Mary K. "Vocabulary Load of Certain State-Adopted Mathematics Textbooks, Grades 1–3," Doctoral dissertation, University of Southern California, Abstract No. 3706, January 1966.

Stern, Catherine. *Children Discover Arithmetic*. New York, N.Y.: Harper & Row, Inc., 1949.

Westcott, Alvin, and James Smith. *Creative Teaching of Mathematics in the Elementary School*. Boston, Mass.: Allyn and Bacon, Inc., 1967.

IV
For All of Us

23

A Declaration on Human Rights and Responsibilities

This Declaration, prepared by members of the Center on Human Policy, Syracuse University, is a strong statement of ideals both for people who have handicaps and for society in general. It touches on many of the goals and opportunities that this book advocates. And it is more important for us to work cooperatively for constructive changes than it is to agree on every principle. How would you feel about signing it?

I freely sign this declaration affirming the constitutional right of anyone to make public one's individual beliefs, irrespective of that person's affiliations or the auspices under which that person is employed. I act now as an independent citizen, representing neither agencies nor others but myself, dedicated in support of these beliefs:

> that, as human beings, all people are inherently valuable;
> that all people have essential rights and privileges;

that, included in these rights, all people must have access
to a broad spectrum of services and opportunities to
insure their physically, spiritually, socially, and psychologically optimum development;

that such development is enhanced in integrated open
community settings;

that among those who have been most frequently detained
in segregated settings, and who have most often been
denied their basic rights, are devalued people with
special needs—the so-called handicapped (e.g., physically disabled, mentally retarded, emotionally disturbed), the elderly, and the disadvantaged.

Therefore, because I support the above statements, I pledge to
work to achieve the following goals:

State and local priorities and allocations shall be designed
and implemented to encourage the creation of sufficient
options to make it possible for all people who are legally
entitled to their freedom to lead integrated and purpose-
ful lives.

Relevant agencies and individuals shall provide support for
the fullest community integration by working toward a
moratorium on the planning, construction, purchase, or
endorsement of any segregated or closed settings that
deprive people of free access to share in community
services. This goal requires enunciation because community priorities and resources heretofore have been primarily designated for segregated facilities.

State and local public and private tax-exempt agencies
shall feel obligated to present regularly to the people
their plans created to insure the fullest community
integration of their clients with special needs. Included
with such plans shall be time estimates for the achievement of their objectives, descriptions of special efforts

that have been made to promote integration, and evaluation summaries of program progress.

That, because all people have a right and a need to achieve, and are guaranteed access to such opportunities by the elements of due process, state and local agencies shall agree that laws are for all people and must be applied justly to everyone, and present discriminatory laws and practices shall be eliminated.

Therefore, because I believe in the natural rights of all people to freedom within just laws and for full opportunities to develop, I will work to achieve the following related provisions, whether such efforts require legislation, litigation, or program implementation:

Human service agencies shall be accountable to their constituents in ways that shall insure that: in both planning and evaluation there shall be clear and well-marked lines of such accountability; providers of services shall not be the sole planners and evaluators of those same services; the primary sources of program planning and evaluation shall be derived from the local community, with substantial consumer participation; there shall be identifiable mechanisms for monitoring and insuring quality of human services; agencies shall be evaluated according to their abilities to demonstrate growing responsiveness to the needs of those whom they serve; detailed information on the general operation of human services will be publicly disseminated and readily accessible, with proper protection of individual privacy. Prudence shall be used in limiting access of third parties to confidential materials in personal records while, at the same time, consumers or their specified agents shall not be prevented access to their own records.

Citizens who seek human services shall be provided with a

series of accessible and appropriate options, from which
they shall be free to select.

Consumers or providers of services who raise questions or
criticisms regarding accountability, discrimination, due
process of the laws, treatment, or related issues shall not
be subjected to retaliatory actions.

Any individual affected by a decision will be involved in
the process of that decision-making. A person unable to
act positively to advance one's own interests shall be
represented by a person pleading the cause of the
individual as if it was his or her own.

Funding shall be dependent upon the ability of agencies to
demonstrate the above principles.

A reasonable proportion of all funding shall be allocated to
support innovative programming sponsored by either
established or emerging agencies.

Recognizing that we, in our society, too often compromise our
human values by treating people unjustly, and recognizing my
responsibilities to myself and others, I pledge dedication in my
daily life to working for the support and realization of these
values and goals.

V

Resources

24

Organizations of Interest to People Who Have a Handicap

Most of the national organizations directly involved with people who have handicaps have been included except groups relating only to veterans (we apologize to those we missed). See also Chapter 25.

AFL-CIO Department of Community Services
   815 16th St., N.W.
   Washington, D.C. 20006
     Rehabilitation of the mentally and physically handicapped, counseling, community health, consumer information.
Alexander Graham Bell Association for the Deaf, Inc.
   3417 Volta Place
   Washington, D.C. 20007
Allergy Foundation of America
   801 Second Ave.
   New York, N.Y. 10017
American Academy for Cerebral Palsy
   1255 New Hampshire Ave., N.W.
   Washington, D.C. 20036

American Academy of Child Psychiatry
  100 Memorial Drive
  Suite 2–9B
  Cambridge, Mass. 02142
American Academy of Pediatrics
  1801 Hinman Ave.
  Evanston, Ill. 60204
American Association for Health, Physical Education and Recreation
    Program for the Handicapped
  National Education Association
  1201 16th St.
  Washington, D.C. 20036
American Association on Mental Deficiency
  5201 Connecticut Ave., N.W.
  Washington, D.C. 20015
    Developmental disabilities, retardation, seminars, and workshops.
    Publications: *Mental Retardation*; *American Journal of Mental Deficiency*
American Association of Psychiatric Services for Children
  250 West 57th St.
  New York, N.Y. 10019
American Association of Workers for the Blind, Inc.
  424 Investment Building
  1511 K St., N.W.
  Washington, D.C.
American Cancer Society
  219 East 42nd St.
  New York, N.Y. 10017
American Civil Liberties Union
  22 East 40th St.
  New York, N.Y. 10016
American Coalition for Citizens with Disabilities
  c/o Center for Concerned Engineering
  1224 DuPont Circle Bldg.
  Washington, D.C. 20036
American Congress of Rehabilitation Medicine
  30 North Michigan Ave.
  Chicago, Ill. 60602
    Provides communication among rehabilitation disciplines, education,
    career placement.
    Publications: *Archives of Physical Medicine*; *Rehabilitation*; *Rehab
    Congress News*

American Diabetes Association
  1 West 48th St.
  New York, N.Y. 10020
American Epilepsy Society
  Bldg. 10, Room 4N262
  National Institute of Health
  Bethesda, Md. 20014
American Foundation for the Blind
  15 West 16th St.
  New York, N.Y. 10011
American Foundation for Learning Disabilities
  P.O. Box 196
  Convent Station, N.J. 07961
American Genetic Association
  1028 Connecticut Ave., N.W.
  Washington, D.C. 20036
American Heart Association
  44 East 23rd St.
  New York, N.Y. 10016
The American Institute of Architects
  7315 Wisconsin Ave., N.W.
  Washington, D.C. 20014
    For information on architectural barriers.
The American Legion
  National Rehabilitation Commission
  1608 K St., N.W.
  Washington, D.C. 20006
American Leprosy Missions, Inc.
  297 Park Ave. South
  New York, N.Y. 10019
    Publication: *News from ALM*
American Library Association
  Library Services to Exceptional Children
  50 East Huron St.
  Chicago, Ill. 60611
American National Red Cross
  17th and D Streets, N.W.
  Washington, D.C. 20006
    Community health and safety programs, service programs for youth.
    Publications: *The Red Cross Youth News; The Good Neighbor*
    Write for catalog of other pamphlets, brochures, etc.

American Orthotic and Prosthetic Association
  1440 N St., N.W.
  Washington, D.C. 20005
    Health care services and rehabilitation for orthopedically handicapped.
  Publications: *Orthotica and Prosthetics; The AOPA Almanac* (monthly)
American Osteopathic Association
  212 East Ohio St.
  Chicago, Ill. 60611
    Public health, health care and services, educational materials.
American Physical Therapy Association
  1156 15th St., N.W.
  Washington, D.C. 20005
    Education, practice and research in conferences, seminars, etc.
    Publications: *Physical Therapy Journal; Progress Report Newsletter; Government Relations Newsletter; Socioeconomics Documents A, B, C* (updated as needed); various technical books
American Podiatry Association
  20 Chevy Chase Circle
  Washington, D.C. 20015
    Involve podiatrists in handicapped programs, information dissemination.
    Publication: *Journal of the American Podiatry Association*
American Printing House for the Blind, Inc.
  1839 Frankfort Ave.
  Louisville, Ky. 40206
    Special educational materials for the blind, research into literature and appliances.
    Publications: Catalogs; informational brochures
American Psychiatric Association
  1700 18th St., N.W.
  Washington, D.C. 20009
American Psychological Association
  Division 22, Psychological Aspects of Disability
  1200 17th St., N.W.
  Washington, D.C. 20036
American School Health Association
  Kent, Ohio 44240
    Publishes a valuable guide entitled *A Directory of National Organizations Concerned with School Health*
American Speech and Hearing Association
  9030 Old Georgetown Road
  Washington, D.C. 20014

Arthritis Foundation
   1212 Avenue of the Americas
   New York, N.Y. 10036
Association for Children with Learning Disabilities
   5225 Grace St.
   Pittsburgh, Pa. 15236
Association for Education of Visually Handicapped
   1604 Spruce St.
   Philadelphia, Pa. 19103
Association of Junior Leagues, Inc.
   825 Third Ave.
   New York, N.Y. 10022
      Promotes volunteering in many capacities.
      Publications: *The Junior League Magazine*; *Annual Report*
Bureau of Education for the Handicapped
   Office of Education
   U.S. Department of HEW
   Washington, D.C. 20202
      Divisions of: Educational Services; Training Programs; Research; Library
         Programs; Special Education
California Association for Neurologically Handicapped Children
   P.O. Box 604
   Los Angeles, Calif. 90053
Center on Human Policy
   216 Ostrom Ave.
   Syracuse, N.Y. 13210
      Publications: Notes from the Center, including:
      No. 2 *Observing in Institutions.* Robert Bogdan (second printing, 1974)
      No. 3 *Children with Special Needs and New York State Educational Law.*
         Elizabeth C. Smith (1973)
      No. 4 *The Financial Issue in Education of the Handicapped.* Daniel D.
         Sage, Joseph G. Gaughan, and Russell G. Rice (1973)
      No. 5 *The Future of Social Policy for Children.* Edward Zigler (1973)
      No. 6 *Sexual Rights for the People . . . Who Happen to Be Handicapped.*
         Sol Gordon (1974)
      No. 7 *Group Homes: One Alternative.* Robert Goodfellow (1974)
Center for Law and Social Policy
   1600 20th St., N.W.
   Washington, D.C. 20009
Center for Multiply Handicapped Children
   105 East 106th St.

New York, N.Y. 10029
> Educational, remedial, and habilitative services for children aged 4 to 7 with more than one disability.

Committee for the Handicapped
People to People Program
1146 16th St., N.W.
Washington, D.C. 20036
> For their publications *Successful Disabled Persons International*, *Directory of Organizations Interested in the Handicapped*, as well as many educational and service-related programs.

Coordinating Council for Handicapped Children
407 South Dearborn St.
Chicago, Ill. 60605

Council for Exceptional Children (CEC)
1920 Association Drive
Reston, Va. 22091
> Publications:
> *Digest of State and Federal Laws: Education of Handicapped Children*
> *Instructional Alternatives for Exceptional Children*
> *Mainstream Special Education*
> *State Laws and Education of Handicapped Children: Issues and Recommendations*
>
> Plus these tape cassettes:
> *Facilitating Change*
> *Leadership of District Administrators*
> *Mainstreaming: What Is It?*
> *Planning at the State Level*
> *Resource Rooms*
> *Teachers Helping Teachers*

Council of National Organizations for Children and Youth
c/o National Committee for Children and Youth, #312
1401 K St., N.W.
Washington, D.C. 20005

Council of Organizations Serving the Deaf
P.O. Box 894
Columbia, Md. 21044
> Visual aids and printed material, public information programs, services for the deaf (legal counseling, adult education, driver safety, vocational training).
> Publications: Annual Forum proceedings, newsletters, and directories

Department of Health, Education, and Welfare, Washington, D.C. 20201
  Children's Bureau
    Division of Health Services
    Division of Social Services
  Division of Welfare Services
  Office of Education
    Bureau of Education for the Handicapped
    Education for Exceptional Children
  Office of Vocational Rehabilitation
  Public Health Service
    National Cancer Institute
    National Heart Institute
    National Institutes of Health
    National Institute of Arthritis and Metabolic Diseases
    National Institute of Mental Health
    National Institute of Neurological Diseases and Blindness
  Social Security Administration
  Bureau of Family Services
Division of Developmental Disabilities
  Room 3062, Mary Switzer Bldg.
  330 C St., S.W.
  Washington, D.C. 20201
Epilepsy Foundation of America
  1828 L St., N.W.
  Washington, D.C. 20036
ERIC Document Reproduction Service
  The National Cash Register Co.
  4936 Fairmount Ave.
  Bethesda, Md. 20014
    Reprints of many articles from journals, magazines.
Federal Housing Administration
  U.S. Dept. of Housing and Urban Development
  Washington, D.C.
    Assists non- or limited-profit or cooperative entities in providing new or
      rehabilitated rented and coop housing for lower-income families.
      Housing may be designed primarily for use by elderly or handicapped
      families and individuals.
Federation for the Handicapped, Inc.
  211 West 14th St.
  New York, N.Y. 10011

Goodwill Industries of America, Inc.
  9200 Wisconsin Ave.
  Washington, D.C. 20014
Industrial Home for the Blind
  57 Willoughby St.
  Brooklyn, N.Y. 11201
Institute for the Crippled and Disabled
  400 First Ave.
  New York, N.Y. 10010
International Association of Laryngectomies
  219 East 42nd St.
  New York, N.Y. 10017
    For people whose larynxes have been removed, with loss of their natural
      voices. Provides free speech lessons, workshops, and public informa-
      tion. Publishes the *I.A.L. News* and helpful pamphlets.
International Association of Parents of the Deaf (IAPD)
  814 Thayer Ave.
  Silver Springs, Md. 20910
International Society for Rehabilitation of the Disabled
  219 East 44th St.
  New York, N.Y. 10017
Leukemia Society of America, Inc.
  211 East 43rd St.
  New York, N.Y. 10017
Medic Alert Foundation International
  1000 North Palm
  Turlock, Calif. 95380
    Provides medical identification emblems (necklace or bracelet) with a
      person's medical problem engraved on it (e.g., allergy to penicillin).
Muscular Dystrophy Associations of America, Inc.
  810 Seventh Ave.
  New York, N.Y. 10019
    Research, patient, and community services.
Myasthenia Gravis Foundation
  155 East 23rd St.
  New York, N.Y. 10010
National Amputation Foundation
  12–45 150th St.
  Whitestone, N.Y. 11357
National Association of Hearing and Speech Agencies
  919 18th St., N.W.
  Washington, D.C. 20006

National Association for Mental Health
    1800 North Kent St.
    Rosslyn, Va. 22209
National Association for Music Therapy, Inc.
    P.O. Box 610
    Lawrence, Kans. 66044
        Use of music in restoring, maintaining, and improving mental and
        physical health.
        Publication: *Journal of Music Therapy*
National Association of the Physically Handicapped, Inc.
    6473 Grandville
    Detroit, Mich. 48228
National Association for Visually Handicapped (partially seeing)
    3201 Balboa St.
    San Francisco, Calif. 94121
National Center for Child Advocacy
    Dept. of HEW, Office of the Secretary
    P.O. Box 1182
    Washington, D.C. 20013
National Center for Law and the Handicapped, Inc.
    1235 North Eddy St.
    South Bend, Ind. 46617
        Actively supports legal rights of all people who have handicaps through
        legal assistance, research, and public and professional education.
        (Write for free *NCLH Newsline* newsletter.)
National Center for Volunteer Action
    1735 I St., N.W.
    Washington, D.C. 20006
National Clearinghouse for Legal Services
    Northwestern University Law School
    710 North Lake Shore Drive
    Chicago, Ill. 60611
National Committee for Children and Youth
    1145 19th St., N.W.
    Washington, D.C. 20036
National Committee for Multi-Handicapped Children
    339 14th St.
    Niagra Falls, N.Y. 14303
National Congress of Organizations of the Physically Handicapped, Inc.
    7611 Oakland Ave.
    Minneapolis, Minn. 55423

A coalition which promotes equal employment rights, legislation, social activity, and rehabilitation.

Publications: *COPH Bulletin*; brochures

National Cystic Fibrosis Research Foundation
3379 Peach Tree Rd., N.E.
Atlanta, Ga. 30326

National Easter Seal Society for Crippled Children and Adults
2023 West Ogden Ave.
Chicago, Ill. 60612

National Epilepsy League, Inc.
116 South Michigan Ave.
Chicago, Ill. 60603

National Foundation (For Birth Defects)
800 Second Ave.
New York, N.Y. 10017
Formerly March of Dimes.

National Foundation for Neuromuscular Diseases
150 West 57th St.
New York, N.Y. 10019

National Hemophilia Foundation
25 West 39th St.
New York, N.Y. 10018
Has prevention, treatment, rehabilitation programs, and community education.

Publication: *Hemofax*

National Institute of Child Health and Human Development
National Institute of Health
Bethesda, Md. 20014

National Institute of Mental Health
Health Services and Mental Health Administration
Chevy Chase, Md. 20015
Divisions of Research; Manpower and Training Programs; Community Mental Health Centers; Communications.

National Institute of Neurological Diseases and Stroke
National Institute of Health
Bethesda, Md. 20014

National Kidney Foundation
116 East 27th St.
New York, N.Y. 10016
Research, patient and community services, donor program.

Publications: *The Kidney*, and educational brochures

National Multiple Sclerosis Society
   257 Park Ave. South
   New York, N.Y. 10010
National Odd Shoe Exchange
   Ruth Feldman
   1415 Ocean Front
   Santa Monica, Calif. 90401
      If you have one foot, or feet of different sizes.
National Paraplegia Foundation
   333 North Michigan Ave.
   Chicago, Ill. 60601
National Safety Council
   425 Michigan Ave.
   Chicago, Ill. 60611
      Prevention of accidents in all areas of life. Publishes eight magazines and
      maintains a large library of accident-prevention information.
National Society for Autistic Children, Inc.
   621 Central Ave.
   Albany, N.Y. 12206
National Tuberculosis and Respiratory Disease Association
   1740 Broadway
   New York, N.Y. 10019
Orton Society
   Box 153
   Pomfret, Conn. 06258
      Workshops, services, and education for the learning disabled.
Partners of the Americas
   2001 S St., N.W.
   Washington, D.C. 20009
SIECUS (Sex Information and Education Council of the U.S.)
   1855 Broadway
   New York, N.Y. 10023
      Devoted to an improved understanding of human sexuality as an aspect
      of individual and social health. Provides professional training and
      information concerning sex education programs and materials.
Sister Kenny Institute
   1800 Chicago Ave.
   Minneapolis, Minn. 55404
Social Advocates for Youth
   315 Montgomery St., Suite 1014
   San Francisco, Calif. 94104

Society for the Rehabilitation of the Facially Disfigured
    550 First Ave.
    New York, N.Y. 10016
United Cerebral Palsy Association, Inc.
    66 East 34th St.
    New York, N.Y. 10016
Youth Organizations United
    912 Sixth St., N.W.
    Washington, D.C. 20001

25

Work Opportunities

Organizations

This list is composed mainly of national organizations and agencies that can in many cases put you in touch with resources in your local area. Some of them sound similar, but they offer different services.

American Association for Rehabilitation Therapy, Inc.
    P.O. Box 93
    North Little Rock, Ark. 72116
American Corrective Therapy Association
    1781 Begen Ave.
    Mountain View, Calif. 94040
        Enhances the health of the handicapped in schools, hospitals, rehab centers, and nursing homes through corrective therapy and physical education.
American Occupational Therapy Association, Inc.
    6000 Executive Blvd., Suite 200
    Rockville, Md. 20852

American Rehabilitation Counseling Association
   1607 New Hampshire Ave., N.W.
   Washington, D.C. 20009
American Rehabilitation Foundation, Inc.
   1900 Chicago Ave.
   Minneapolis, Minn. 55404
American Vocational Association
   1510 H St., N.W.
   Washington, D.C. 20036
     For information on your career interests.
Bureau of Apprenticeship and Training
   Manpower Administration
   U.S. Dept. of Labor
   Washington, D.C. 20210
     For literature and information in your field of interest. Also ask for the
       location of your regional office, which supplies the names of firms in
       your area that offer apprenticeship training programs.
Bureau of Labor Statistics
   U.S. Dept. of Labor
   Washington, D.C. 20210
     For information on most careers and occupations.
Careers
   Washington, D.C. 20202
Council of State Administrators of Vocational Rehabilitation
   1522 K St., N.W.
   Suite 836
   Washington, D.C. 20005
     Supervision of vocational rehabilitation of physically and mentally
       handicapped persons in the major federal agencies.
     Publications: *CSAVR Memorandum*; other reports and manuals
Department of Human Resources Development
   Mail Control Unit
   800 Capitol Mall
   Sacramento, Calif. 95814
     Has much free information and literature in a wide variety of occupa-
       tions.
Department of Vocational Education
   1201 16th St., N.W.
   Washington, D.C. 20036
EPI-HAB, L.A., Inc.
   5533 South Western Ave.

Los Angeles, Calif. 90062
Medical control, work training, employment, and placement of the person with epilepsy.

Publications: *Exploring the Work Potential of the Unemployed Epileptic*; *How to Live with Epilepsy*; *Living with Epileptic Seizures*; *Total Rehabilitation of Epileptics*; magazines, feature stories, journals, pamphlets, dissertations

Federation Employment and Guidance Service
215 Park Ave. South
New York, N.Y. 10003

Job placement, educational and vocational guidance, vocational rehabilitation, skills training, psychological testing and remedial services for the socially, emotionally, and physically handicapped.

Publications: Numerous articles, pamphlets, guides, and directories (bibliography available on request)

Goodwill Industries of America
9200 Wisconsin Ave.
Washington, D.C. 20014

Vocational rehabilitation services, training, employment, and opportunities for personal growth for the handicapped, disabled, and disadvantaged.

Publications: *Newsletter*; *A.I.M.*; *Advance*; *Annual Report*; *Annual Statistical Report*

ICD Rehabilitation and Research Center
340 East 24th St.
New York, N.Y. 10010

Rehabilitation treatment and training, research and professional education.

Publications: Quarterly newsletter; general-purpose descriptive brochures; *Annual Report*; professional publications

International Association of Rehabilitation Facilities, Inc.
5530 Wisconsin Ave., #955
Washington, D.C. 20015

Assists in the development and improvement of medically oriented rehabilitation centers and sheltered workshops.

Publications: *FOCUS on Facilities*; periodical Educational Series Reports

National Association of Sheltered Workshops
1522 K St., N.W.
Washington, D.C. 20005

National Committee on Employment of Youth of the National Child Labor Committee

145 East 32nd St.

New York, N.Y. 10016

National Industries for the Blind

1455 Broad St.

Bloomfield, N.J. 07003

Coordinates workshops, consumer information

Publications: *Annual Report*; *Inside NIB*: *Directory of Workshops*

National Institutes of Rehabilitation and Health Services

1714 Massachusetts Ave., N.W.

Washington, D.C. 20036

National Rehabilitation Association

1522 K Street, N.W.

Washington, D.C. 20005

Works toward the welfare and rehabilitation of all handicapped people.

Publication: *Journal of Rehabilitation*

National Vocational Guidance Association

1607 New Hampshire Ave., N.W.

Washington, D.C. 20009

For "Career Decision" and other assistance.

Office of Education

U.S. Department of HEW

400 Maryland Ave., S.W.

Washington, D.C. 20202

For vocational and technical education opportunities.

The President's Committee on the Employment of the Handicapped

Washington, D.C. 20210

Rehabilitation Gazette

4502 Maryland Ave.

St. Louis, Mo. 63108

Rehabilitation International

219 East 44th St.

New York, N.Y. 10017

Rehabilitation Services Administration

Social and Rehabilitation Service, U.S. DHEW

330 Independence Ave., S.W.

Washington, D.C. 20201

Supports a wide range of state rehabilitative services for disabled persons. Funding for construction and advancement of facilities. The RSA administers research-grant programs to improve rehab techniques. For information on the Vocational Rehabilitation Act of 1973.

Small Business Administration

1441 L St., N.W., Imperial Bldg.

Washington, D.C. 20416

  For information on loans up to $350,000 at 3 percent interest for handicapped individuals to establish small businesses and nonprofit workshops for the handicapped (P.L. 92-595, The Small Business Investment Act Amendments of 1972).

Social and Rehabilitation Service

  330 C St., S.W.

  Washington, D.C. 20201

Society for Occupational Research Ltd.

  1860 Broadway

  New York, N.Y. 10023

U.S. Civil Service Commission

  1900 E St., N.W.

  Washington, D.C. 20415

  Write for lists of publications on employment of physically handicapped.

U.S. Office of Education

  Division of Vocational and Technical Education

  Washington, D.C. 20202

Literature

Career Education: Exemplary Programs for the Handicapped

  available from The Council for Exceptional Children

  1920 Association Drive

  Reston, Va. 22091

The Guide to Career Education by Muriel Lederer. New York: Quadrangle/ The New York Times Book Co., 1974. Very thorough in describing most jobs and professions, including where to go for assistance.

An Index to Rehabilitation and Social Service Projects, Volume II (1955–1973)

from: Regional Rehabilitation Research Institute

  College of Health Related Professions

  J. Hillis Miller Health Center

  Gainesville, Fla. 32610

Mental Health Jobs Today and Tomorrow by Elizabeth Ogg

from: Public Affairs Pamphlets

  381 Park Ave. South

  New York, N.Y. 10016

Briefly describes social workers, family therapists, group workers, mental health nurses, psychiatrists, psychologists, and other professions. Many other helpful pamphlets are available in this series.

New Readers Press

1320 Jamesville Ave.

Syracuse, N.Y. 13210

For publications for people with limited reading ability including: *Occupations, Occupations 2, Finding a Job, The World of Work.*

Selected Career Education Programs for the Handicapped

Superintendent of Documents

U.S. Government Printing Office

Washington, D.C. 20402

Ask for other publications relevant to your situation.

Vocational Guidance Manuals

235 East 45th St.

New York, N.Y. 10017

Offers guides to many fields of interest.

26

Media

Books—A Selected List

Ayrault, Evelyn West. *Helping the Handicapped Teenager Mature.* New York: Association Press, 1971. Age twelve to young adult. Deals primarily with daily problems and young person's role in home and society. A broad range of handicapping conditions.

Barnes, Ellen, Bill Eyman, and Maddy Bragar Engoly. *Teach and Reach—An Alternative to Resources for the Classroom.* Syracuse, N.Y.: Human Policy Press, 1974. Teachers as advocates, problem solvers, risk takers. Gets teachers in touch with their own feelings and those of students.

Biklen, Douglas. *Let Our Children Go—An Organizing Manual for Advocates and Parents.* Syracuse, N.Y.: Human Policy Press, 1974. Talks about tactics for obtaining rights, how to communicate.

Blatt, Burton. *Souls in Extremis.* Boston: Allyn and Bacon, 1973. A poetic cry for justice!

Brutten, Milton, Sylvia O. Richardson, and Charles Mangel. *Something's Wrong with My Child.* New York: Harcourt Brace Jovanovich, Inc., 1973.

Use of case studies in a humanistic book written in a personal style emphasizing the home, school, and general management of the learning disabled.

Buscaglia, Leo. *The Disabled and Their Parents: A Counseling Challenge.* Thorofare, N.J.: Charles B. Slack, Inc., 1975. With contributions from various authors, it encourages parents, students, and professionals to accept cooperative responsibility.

Gordon, Sol. *Facts About Sex for Today's Youth.* Rev. ed. New York: John Day, 1973. Illustrated and written in simple terms, it deals with areas of prime concern for adolescents.

————. *Facts About VD for Today's Youth.* New York: John Day, 1973. Illustrated, explains contraction, treatment, and prevention in teens' own words.

————. *Let's Make Sex a Household Word.* New York: John Day, 1975. A book to help parents sex-educate their children and to understand their own sexuality.

Gregory, Martha Ferguson. *Sexual Adjustment—A Guide for the Spinal Cord Injured.* Bloomington, Ill.: Accent Publications, 1973.

Heslinga, K., *Not Made of Stone—The Sexual Problems of Handicapped People.* Springfield, Ill.: Charles C. Thomas, Publisher, 1974. Takes a very helping, practical (illustrated) position for many handicapping conditions.

Hobbes, Nicholas, and colleagues. Final report, *The Futures of Children,* and two volumes of task-force papers, *Issues in the Classification of Children.* San Francisco: Jossey-Bass, Inc., 1974. Endorses the principle of classifying to open opportunities and rejects labeling that is an end in itself or that doesn't serve children's needs. Its first priority is shifting from helping the handicapped per se to helping families help children.

Kratoville, Betty Lou, ed. *Youth in Trouble.* San Rafael, Calif.: Academic Therapy Publications, 1974. The best review of the relationship between delinquency and learning disability. A call to action.

Kronick, Doreen. *A Word or Two About Learning Disabilities.* San Rafael, Calif.: Academic Therapy Publications, 1973. Urges involved family members and professionals to communicate, and to maintain a balanced perspective about the learning disability situation.

Kvaraceus, William C. and E. Nelson Hayes. *If Your Child Is Handicapped.* Boston: Porter Sargent, 1969. A collection of autobiographical reports from parents of handicapped children.

Levy, Harold B., M.D. *Square Pegs, Round Holes.* Boston and Toronto: Little, Brown and Co., 1973. Advocates an LD team comprised of parents, teachers, and professionals; fairly intellectually written.

Paterson, George W. *Helping Your Handicapped Child.* Minneapolis, Minn.: Augsburg Publishing House, 1975. This book shows how parents can meet the child's needs, use community resources, and gain strength through faith.

Siegel, Ernest. *The Exceptional Child Grows Up.* New York: E. P. Dutton & Co., Inc., 1974. Focuses on the persisting problems of learning-disabled adolescents and young adults.

Spock, Benjamin, and Marion O. Lerrigo. *Caring for Your Disabled Child.* Greenwich, Conn.: Fawcett Publications, Inc., 1965. Medical care and rehabilitation, education, recreation, sexuality, daily living, sound advice for parents of children with mental, physical, or emotional handicaps.

Waldhorn, Hilda K. *Rehabilitation of the Physically Handicapped Adolescent.* New York: John Day, 1973. Sections on epilepsy, hemophilia, sickle cell anemia, diabetes, allergies and asthma, brain injury, for nonmedical personnel.

Directories

Directory for Exceptional Children. Porter Sargent, Publisher.

Directory of Facilities for the Learning Disabled and Handicapped. Harper & Row.

Directory of Organizations Interested in the Handicapped. Committee for the Handicapped, Suite 610, La Salle Bldg., Connecticut Ave. and L St., Washington, D.C. 20036.

Encyclopedia of Associations. Gale Research Co.

Write for Catalogs

Academic Therapy Publications
   1539 Fourth St.
   San Rafael, Calif. 94901
Charles C. Thomas
   301–327 East Lawrence Ave.
   Springfield, Ill. 62717
Fearon Publishers
   6 Davis Drive
   Belmont, Calif. 94002

John Day Co.
  666 Fifth Ave.
  New York, N.Y. 10019
Interpretive Education
  400 Bryant St.
  Kalamazoo, Mich. 49001
Laubach Literacy, Inc.
  Box 131
  Syracuse, N.Y. 13210
Love Publishing Co.
  6635 East Villanova Pl.
  Denver, Colo. 80222
Special Child Publications
  Bernie Straub Publishing Co., Inc.
  4535 Union Bay Place, N.E.
  Seattle, Wash. 98105

Pamphlets

Coordinating Council for Exceptional Children. *How to Organize an Effective Parent Group and Move Bureaucracies.* Coordinating Council for Exceptional Children, 407 South Dearborn, Chicago, Ill. 60605. Detailed step-by-step, how to deal with barriers and appeal, methods of protest, etc.

Coordinating Council for Exceptional Children. *Your Guide to Services of Handicapped Children.* Coordinating Council for Exceptional Children, 407 South Dearborn, Chicago, Ill. 60605. Private schools, camps, mental health centers, parent groups, clinics, state institutions, private and public agencies.

Coordinating Council for Exceptional Children. *Your Rights as Parents of a Handicapped Child.* Coordinating Council for Exceptional Children, 407 South Dearborn, Chicago, Ill. 60605. Explains provisions of the Mandatory Special Education Law and the Tuition Reimbursement Law, and steps to obtain services.

Golick, Margaret. *A Parent's Guide to Learning Problems.* Quebec: Quebec ACLD, 1970.

Hodgeman, Karen, and Eleanor Warpeha. *Adaptations and Techniques for the Disabled Homemaker.* Minneapolis, Minn.: Sister Kenny Institute, 1973. Illustrated methods to cook, clean, adapt utensils and appliances, maneuver around.

Miller, Julano. *Helping Your LD Child at Home*. San Rafael, Calif.: Academic Therapy Publications, 1973.

Nordqvist, Inger. *Life Together—The Situation of the Handicapped*. Available from:

> The Swedish Central Committee for Rehabilitation
> Fack
> S-161 03 Bromma 3
> Sweden

Sackmary, Arnold, and Roger Zeeman. *Special People*. Convent Station, N.J.: New Jersey ACLD. Written for siblings of the handicapped, to help them understand special home and school considerations.

Generally, these pamphlets offer daily, practical suggestions for developing and encouraging a child's capabilities. The ones by Ahr and Simon, Golick, and Miller focus on learning disabilities, and Nordqvist's deals primarily with physically handicapped.

Very Special New Idea

For people who don't like to read much or who have limited vocabularies. *Shazam*, *Batman*, and *Superman* presented as aids to reading.

Write: Edugraphics, National Periodical Publication, Inc., 75 Rockefeller Plaza, New York, N.Y. 10019

Visual Aids

American Documentary Films
379 Bay St.
San Francisco, Calif. 94133
American Documentary Films
336 West 84th St.
New York, N.Y. 10024
Association of Instructional Materials
866 Third Ave.
New York, N.Y. 10022
BFA (Bailey Films Associates)
2211 Michigan Ave.
Santa Monica, Calif. 90404

Contemporary Films
   267 West 25th St.
   New York, N.Y. 10001
Educational Activities, Inc.
   P.O. Box 392
   Freeport, N.Y. 11520
      Getting It Together Is Life Itself, a filmstrip and tape to help young
         people get their heads together.
Films Incorporated
   35-01 Queens Blvd.
   Long Island City, N.Y. 11101
Hallmark Films and Recordings, Inc.
   1511 East North Ave.
   Baltimore, Md. 21213
Impact Films Catalog
   144 Bleecker St.
   New York, N.Y. 10012
Lawren Publications, Inc.
   P.O. Box 1542
   Burlingame, Calif. 94010
      Film *Adolescence and Learning Disabilities.*
Mass Media Ministries
   2116 North Charles St.
   Baltimore, Md. 21218
Media Resources Branch
   National Medical Audiovisual Center (Annex)
   Station K
   Atlanta, Ga. 30324
      Four short films to help quadriplegics become functionally independent
         (driving, dressing, showering and grooming, bowel and bladder tech-
         niques).
Multi-Media Resource Center, Inc.
   540 Powell St.
   San Francisco, Calif. 94108
      Touching and other films.
National Audiovisual Center
   Suitland Road
   Suitland, Md. 20023
National Center on Educational Media and Materials for the Handicapped
   College of Education
   Ohio State University

220 West 12th Ave.

Columbus, Ohio 43210

    Available are a publications list and newsletter. Learning resources, educational technology, and instructional programs.

NICEM (National Information Center for Educational Media)

University of Southern California

University Park

Los Angeles, Calif. 90007

Pacific Tape Library

2217 Shattuck Ave.

Berkeley, Calif. 94704

Perennial Films

1825 Willow Rd.

Northfield, Ill. 60093

    Like Other People and other films and filmstrips.

Regional Media Centers for the Deaf

New Mexico State University

Box 3AW

Las Cruces, N.M. 88003

Sister Kenny Institute

1800 Chicago Ave.

Minneapolis, Minn. 55404

SWANK Motion Pictures, Inc.

2151 Marion Place

Baldwin, N.Y. 11510

Tricontinental Film Cinema

244 West 27th St.

New York, N.Y. 10001

Universal Education and Visual Arts

221 Park Ave. South

New York, N.Y. 10003

University of California Extension Media Center

(EMC)

Berkeley, Calif. 94720

    Good catalog: *Lifelong Learning.*

World Horizon Films

Maryknoll, N.Y. 10545

Periodicals

In addition to these magazines and publications, many of the organizations we list in the chapter titled "Organizations of Interest to the Handicapped" publish newsletters, pamphlets, and other literature.

Academic Therapy
    Academic Therapy Publications
    1539 Fourth St.
    San Rafael, Calif. 94901
Accent on Living
    P.O. Box 726
    Gillum Rd. & High Dr.
    Bloomington, Ill. 61701
        Practical, lively articles and information for people who have handicaps.
American Annals of the Deaf
    Executive Manager
    Conference of Executives of American Schools for the Deaf
    5034 Wisconsin Ave., N.W.
    Washington, D.C. 20016
        A national professional journal for teachers, specialists, and school
            administrators working for education of the deaf.
American Foundation for the Blind Newsletter
    15 West 16th St.
    New York, N.Y. 10011
American Journal of Occupational Therapy
    6000 Executive Blvd.
    Rockville, Md. 20852
A S H A
    American Speech and Hearing Association
    9030 Old Georgetown Rd.
    Washington, D.C. 20014
Brain and Language
    Academic Press, Inc.
    111 Fifth Ave.
    New York, N.Y. 10003
Children Today
    Superintendent of Documents
    U.S. Government Printing Office
    Washington, D.C. 20402

Developmental Medicine and Child Neurology
　J. B. Lippincott Co.
　East Washington Square
　Philadelphia, Pa. 19105
　　Official journal of the American Academy for Cerebral Palsy.
dsh Abstracts
　American Speech and Hearing Association
　9030 Old Georgetown Rd.
　Washington, D.C. 20014
Exceptional Children
　Official Journal of the CEC
　1920 Association Dr.
　Reston, Va. 22091
The Exceptional Parent
　P.O. Box 964
　Manchester, N.H. 03105
　　Practical guidance for parents of children with disabilities.
Focus on Exceptional Children
　6635 East Villanova Pl.
　Denver, Colo. 80222
Hearing
　The Royal National Institute for the Deaf
　105 Gower St.
　London WC1E 6AH
　England
The Independent
　Center for Independent Living, Inc.
　2054 University Ave.
　Berkeley, Calif. 94704
　　A new voice for the disabled and blind.
Journal of Abnormal Child Psychology
　1151 K St., N.W.
　Washington, D.C. 20005
　　Devoted to studies of behavioral pathology in childhood and adolescence.
The Journal of Auditory Research
　Box N
　Groton, Conn. 06340
Journal of Autism and Childhood Schizophrenia
　1151 K St., N.W.
　Washington, D.C. 20005
　　Devoted to all severe psychopathologies in childhood.

Journal of Clinical Child Psychology
   Meramec Bldg.
   111 South Meramec Ave.
   Clayton, Mo. 63105
Journal of Developmental Disabilities
   P.O. Box 8470, Gentilly Station
   New Orleans, La. 70182
      Research and functional articles on the range of problems under
      "developmental disabilities" for involved professionals.
Journal of Learning Disabilities
   Executive Office
   The Professional Press, Inc.
   Room 1410
   5 South Wabash Ave.
   Chicago, Ill. 60602
      Multidisciplinary, clinical exchange, international.
The Journal of Special Education
   Grune & Stratton, Inc.
   111 Fifth Ave.
   New York, N.Y. 10003
Journal of Speech and Hearing Disorders
Journal of Speech and Hearing Research
   Both from: American Speech and Hearing Association
                  9030 Old Georgetown Rd.
                  Washington, D.C. 20014
The New Outlook for the Blind
   American Foundation for the Blind, Inc.
   15 West 16th St.
   New York, N.Y. 10011
Paraplegia News
   7315 Wisconsin Ave.
   Washington, D.C. 20014
The Personnel and Guidance Journal
   American Personnel and Guidance Association
   1607 New Hampshire Ave., N.W.
   Washington, D.C. 20009
The Pointer
   New Readers Press
   1320 Jamesville Ave.
   Box 131
   Syracuse, N.Y. 13210

For special-class teachers and parents of the handicapped.

Rehabilitative Digest
Canadian Rehabilitation Council for the Disabled
1 Yonge St.
Toronto, Canada M5E 1E8

Rehabilitation Literature
National Easter Seal Society for Crippled Children and Adults
2023 West Ogden Ave.
Chicago, Ill. 60612

Teaching Exceptional Children
1411 South Jefferson Davis Hwy.
Suite 900
Arlington, Va. 22202

Therapeutic Recreation Journal
National Therapeutic Recreation Society
National Recreation and Park Association
1601 North Kent St.
Arlington, Va. 22209

The Vocational Guidance Quarterly
American Personnel and Guidance Association
1607 New Hampshire Ave., N.W.
Washington, D.C. 20009

The Volta Review
3417 Volta Place, N.W.
Washington, D.C. 20007

27

Leisure Reading for Young People

If you are just getting interested in reading and want to test it out, start with magazines (*Mad, National Lampoon, Time, Newsweek, U.S. News and World Report, Seventeen, Teen, Essence, Jet, Sports Illustrated*) or read daily newspapers or comic books.

Besides the usual superheroes, these comics have outrageous gags with a message as well:

What Do You Do When You're All Drug Doubt?
Gut News for Modern Eaters
Juice Use—Special Hangover Edition
Protect Yourself from Becoming an Unwanted Parent
Ten Heavy Facts About Sex
VD Claptrap

($2.00 for all six plus publication list from the Institute for Family Research and Education, 760 Ostrom Ave., Syracuse, N.Y. 13210.)

For a new experience in reading, get a copy of *YOU*, a beautifully illustrated survival guide by Sol Gordon which gets into coping with school, parents, boredom, and a few other surprises. Paperback by Quadrangle Books. Join a book club which offers new members several books for practically nothing.

These books are good for people who like to read as well as those getting started:

Catcher in the Rye, J. D. Salinger
The Chosen, Chaim Potok
East of Eden, John Steinbeck
One Flew Over the Cuckoo's Nest, Ken Kesey
The Revised Last Whole Earth Catalog
Siddhartha, Hermann Hesse
The Sun Also Rises, Ernest Hemingway
The science fiction of Ray Bradbury and Arthur C. Clarke
Jack London's books, such as *Sea Wolf*
Books by Mark Twain
In addition, books on the best-seller list are usually fun, although they're
   not always the best literature.

For those who like to read, any novels by:

James Baldwin
John Barth
E. M. Forster
Nikos Kazantzakis
Iris Murdoch
Sylvia Plath
Kurt Vonnegut
Elie Wiesel
Virginia Woolf

Plus these books:

The Bell Jar, Sylvia Plath
Fear of Flying, Erica Jong
I Never Promised You a Rose Garden, Hannah Green
The Teachings of Don Juan (and the rest of the series), Carlos Castaneda

For experiences of self-growth:

The Crack in the Cosmic Egg, Joseph C. Pearce
Guide to Rational Living, Albert Ellis and Robert A. Harper (1975
   edition)
How to Live with a Neurotic, Albert Ellis (1975 edition)

Living with Everyday Problems, Eugene C. Kennedy
Loneliness, Clark E. Moustakas
Love, Leo F. Buscaglia
Psychology for You, Sol Gordon
Transparent Self, Sidney M. Jourard

Inspirational, by someone who is handicapped:

If You Could See What I Hear, Tom Sullivan and Dereck Gill
   As the authors state, this book should "encourage the self-piteous to strive, the hopeless to hang on, the timid to take courage, the cynic to smother his sneer, perhaps even the faithless to quest."

28

The First Full Life Catalogue

Activities

Art Programs

American Industrial Arts Association
    1201 16th St., N.W.
    Washington, D.C. 20036
National Art Education Association
    1201 16th St., N.W.
    Washington, D.C. 20036
    "Careers in Art" and a list of schools with art programs

Astrology

Astrology fascinates many people who have their charts read, read their daily horoscope, and contemplate the signs of the zodiac, predict the future.

Astronomy

Star gaze, identify constellations and planets, learn to work with maps, get a telescope, watch for meteor showers and eclipses.

Bird Watching

Get binoculars and a good bird identification guide. Build a bird feeder and observe the birds that feed. Contact:
The National Audubon Society
   950 Third Ave.
   New York, N.Y. 10022

Building Models

Make ships in bottles, put together remote-controlled boats and airplanes. Design your own models. Custom-cut balsa wood and other materials to make them. Carve soap.

Camping, Residential

Few things are as exhilarating as forests, mountains, and outdoor smells. Write:
American Camping Association
   Bradford Woods
   Martinsville, Ind. 46151
      For information on public camp grounds and programs with facilities for people with handicaps.
National Easter Seal Society
   2023 West Ogden Ave.
   Chicago, Ill. 60612
      For a directory of residential camps for the disabled.

Foot or Mouth Painting

Association of Handicapped Artists, Inc.
   1034 Rand Bldg.
   Buffalo, N.Y. 13203

Gardening

Be a plant person—from houseplants to a big vegetable garden to flower arranging. Learn the names and varieties and characteristics of trees, flowers, and plants. An inexpensive greenhouse is a wise investment for gardening all winter. Terrariums are popular and require a unique skill to make them survive. Bonsai (miniature trees), herb gardens, and organic gardening are other possibilities.

A helpful book:
Gardening for the Handicapped by Betty Massingham
International Collections
P.O. Box 1153
New York, N.Y. 10023

Ham Radio

This puts you in touch with hundreds of other ham enthusiasts. You can help in emergency situations (call the ambulance, police, fire department), play chess or other games over the air, get to know people you can't see.
Join:
The American Radio Relay League (ARRL)
225 Main St.
Newington, Conn. 06111

Magic Tricks

For some starts:
Magic Tricks for Amateurs by W. Dexter
Wehman Brothers
100 Main St.
Hackensack, N.J. 07601
Popular Card Tricks by Walter B. Gibson
Borden Publishing Co.
1855 Main St.
Alhambra, Calif. 91801

Musical Instruments

If you are considering a musical career and have a visual disability, contact:
Louis Braille Foundation for Blind Musicians, Inc.

112 East 19th St.
New York, N.Y. 10003
Music Educators National Conference
1201 16th St., N.W.
Suite 650
Washington, D.C. 20036
  For "Careers in Music" and a list of schools with music departments.

Pen Pals

Accent will pair you with a person of similar interests and age or one with different interests, as pen pals. For information:
Accent Pen Pals
  Box 726
  Bloomington, Ill. 61701
    Include a stamped, self-addressed envelope.
  You can correspond by tapes with people all over the United States and forty countries. Write:
The Voicespondence Club
  P.O. Box 207
  Shillington, Pa. 19607
or write to:
Concerned Youth for Cerebral Palsy
  66 East 34th St.
  New York, N.Y. 10016

Photography

Take pictures and learn to develop and print them yourself. Put together a photo album of your best shots.

Physical Activities

Good, regular exercise not only keeps people more healthy, but makes their bodies and minds more responsive. Try:

  Billiards
  Boating
  Croquet
  Darts

Fishing (electric fishing reels allow persons with limited strength or one arm to fish easily. From: Miza Epoch U.S.A., Inc., P.O. Box 338, Lomita, Calif. 90717)
Isometrics (not for people with high blood pressure)
Miniature Golf
Volleyball

Join the YMCA, YWCA, YMHA, YWHA. Some of these organizations have groups for people with handicaps as well as integrated ones:
National Board of YWCA
600 Lexington Ave.
New York, N.Y. 10022
National Council of the YMCA
291 Broadway
New York, N.Y. 10007
For the addresses of local YMHA's and YWHA's, write:
National Jewish Welfare Board
15 East 26th St.
New York, N.Y. 10010

Blind

You can do many things with a friend. Ride a tandem bicycle, roller or ice skate, run track or cross-country.
For books for the blind and physically handicapped, write:
Division for the Blind and Physically Handicapped
Library of Congress
Washington, D.C. 20542

Indoor Sports Fans

AAHPER Publications-Sales
1201 16th St., N.W.
Washington, D.C. 20036
    Special Olympics Instructional Manual—From Beginners to Champions.
    Also ask for publication list.
Indoor Sports Club
3445 Trumbell St.
San Diego, Calif. 92106
Lea and Febiger

600 Washington Square
Philadelphia, Pa. 19106
Games, Sports and Exercises for the Physically Handicapped by Ronald
   C. Adams
National Therapeutic Recreation Society
1601 North Kent St.
Arlington, Va. 22209

Wheelchair Athletics and Competitions

American Wheelchair Bowling Association
   2635 N.E. 19th St.
   Pompano Beach, Fla. 33062
National Amputee Skiers Association
   863 United Nations Plaza
   New York, N.Y. 10017
      Skiing, water skiing, horseback riding, and trampoline
National Wheelchair Athletic Association
   40-24 62nd St.
   Woodside, N.Y. 11377
      Archery, track and field events, table tennis, swimming, and weight
      lifting
National Wheelchair Basketball Association
   Oak St. at Stadium Drive
   Champaign, Ill. 61820

Recreation Literature

For a good listing of recreation literature from many publishers, including
swimming, camping, art, etc., for all people with handicaps, see the May 1974
issue of:
Focus on Exceptional Children
   6635 East Villanova Place
   Denver, Colo. 80222

Stamp or Coin Collecting

It is interesting to specialize, such as collecting every year of pennies from the various mints, or the Eisenhower series of silver dollars. Proof and uncirculated coin sets and first-day covers of stamps are unusual and valuable pieces as well.

Transcendental Meditation

This should not be confused with any religious movements from India. T.M. claims to be nonreligious. Anyone can learn to meditate in just a few hours of practice for a fee. To learn of the meditation center nearest you, write:
SIMS-IMS National Center
  1015 Gayley Ave.
  Los Angeles, Calif. 90024

Travel

Travel with family, friend, or join a travel group. Disabled persons planning foreign trips can obtain information on transportation, travel facilities, access, and medical services around the world from:
The Central Bureau for Educational Visits and Exchanges
  43 Dorset St.
  London W1H 3FN
  England
  Travel agents who operate tours for people with handicaps in America and abroad:
Evergreen Travel Service, Inc.
  19429 44th St.
  Lynnwood, Wash. 98036
Flying Wheel Tours
  148 West Bridge St.
  Box 382
  Owatonna, Minn. 55060
Grant Travel Consultants
  427 Broad St.
  Shrewsbury, N.J. 07701
Handy-Cap Horizons
  3250 East Loretta Drive
  Indianapolis, Ind. 46227
Hill Travel House
  2628 Fair Oaks Blvd.

Sacramento, Calif. 95825
Kasheta Travel, Inc.
139 Main St.
East Rockaway, N.Y. 11518
Rambling Tours, Inc.
P.O. Box 1304
Hallandale, Fla. 33009

Volunteer Work

Work on a telephone crisis service (such as Contact) talking to upset, lonely,
troubled people. Or get in touch with a volunteer center:
Association of Volunteer Bureaus of America
P.O. Box 7253
Kansas City, Mo. 63113
National Center for Volunteer Action
1735 I St., N.W.
Washington, D.C. 20006

Yoga

As taught by gurus in various disciplines (Kundalini yoga, Hatha yoga, etc.),
yoga is a rejoicing in spiritual and physical enlightenment through meditation,
diet, and exercise. Two good resources for the locations of ashrams (yoga
centers):
Spiritual Community Guide for North America
Spiritual Community
Box 1080
San Rafael, Calif. 94902
Year One Catalog
Harper & Row Publishers, Inc.
10 East 53rd Street
New York, N.Y 10022
These books also list Baha'i centers, T'ai Chi groups, Macrobiotics, Sensory
Awareness, Astrology, Self-Realization, and lots of others.

Miscellaneous

People collect all kinds of things: bottles, fossils, rocks, pressed leaves and
flowers, butterflies and other insects, shells, buttons, dolls.

Join a record, book, art, coin, stamp, gourmet, flower, or anything club—these can help you keep abreast of developments in your field.

Learn to be a gourmet cook or amateur wine taster. Bake bread, pies, cakes. Try exotic recipes from a lot of different countries. Make your own yogurt, cheese, ice cream, bread, wine, or beer. Collect cookbooks, swap recipes, give dinner parties. Try eating vegetarian foods for a while—get a good health food cookbook and visit a natural food store.

Breed dogs, cats, birds, tropical fish, rabbits, hamsters, mice, or gerbils for fun and profit. To take one example, an aquarium will allow you to raise and enjoy tropical fish in a fantasylike underwater world you create yourself. Combinations of sand, rocks, snails, plants, and fish can be varied to suit individual tastes.

Information About Schools and Programs

Closer Look is an information service which was established to help people find services for children with mental, physical, emotional, and learning handicaps. It publishes a newsletter and maintains a mailing list. Upon inquiry, it will provide much information keyed to an individual's handicap and state of residence (Closer Look, Box 1492, Washington, D.C. 20013).

For information about alternative high schools, write:
School of Education
    Indiana University
    Bloomington, Ind. 47401
School of Education
    University of Massachusetts
    Amherst, Mass. 01002

For information on a postgraduate program that creates a professional life for young adults with pronounced learning disabilities, write:
Director, PARA-Education Center, School of Education
    New York University
    1 Washington Place
    New York, N.Y. 10003

For extension and correspondence courses available from regionally accredited colleges and universities, write:
National University Extension Association
    1 DuPont Circle, N.W.
    Suite 360
    Washington, D.C. 20036

Private companies that offer correspondence courses in hundreds of areas
are listed in:
Council of Better Business Bureaus, Inc.
   1150 17th St., N.W.
   Washington, D.C. 20036
      For *Tips on Home Study Schools*, local Bureau addresses, and other
      consumer information.
National Home Study Council
   1601 18th St., N.W.
   Washington, D.C. 20009
   Courses available for rapid reading in Braille. For more information, write:
Vearl G. McBride, Ph.D.
   Culver-Stockton College
   Canton, Mo. 63435

Getting a Job

Getting a Job by Florence Randall
   Lear Siegler, Inc.
   Fearon Publishers
   6 Davis Drive
   Belmont, Calif. 94002
      For people without much experience.

Pamphlets:
25 *Technical Careers*
   Careers
   Washington, D.C. 20202
200 Ways to Put Your Talent to Work in the Health Field
   The National Health Council
   Box 40
   Radio City Station
   New York, N.Y. 10019

Write:
The National Technical Information Service
   Department of Commerce
   Washington, D.C. 20230
      If you are looking for a job overseas.
The Office of Personnel, APN-30

U.S. Dept. of Transportation
Federal Aviation Administration
800 Independence Ave., S.W.
Washington, D.C. 20591
   If you are interested in qualifying as an electronics technician, engineer, or air traffic controller.

Planning for College

American Association of Community and Junior Colleges
   1 DuPont Circle, N.W., Suite 410
   Washington, D.C. 20036
American Association of Specialized Colleges
   P.O. Box 500
   University Park
   Gas City, Ind. 46933
American Association of Theological Schools in the U.S. and Canada
   534 Third National Bldg.
   Dayton, Ohio 45402
American College Admissions Center
   1601 Walnut St.
   Philadelphia, Pa. 19103

Super Newsletters

New Schools Exchange
   Pettigrew, Ark. 72752
   Monthly newsletter and directory of "alternative" schools.
Resources for Youth
   National Commission on Resources for Youth
   36 West 44th St.
   New York, N.Y. 10036
      Information on innovative education programs that stress work/study and student-initiated projects. Files on over 700 programs. Write for sample newsletter.

Problems

Write a letter to *Accent on Living* (P.O. Box 726, Gillum Rd. & High Dr., Bloomington, Ill. 61701) for solutions to problems, such as how to adapt a camera or washing machine to your disability. Find out about hand controls for driving a car, even in a wheelchair.

Civic Action Groups

Alternatives, Interaction Coalition
1500 Farragut St., N.W.
Washington, D.C. 20011
Citizen Action Can Get Results
EPA
Office of Public Affairs
Washington, D.C. 20460

Advocacy

The Center on Human Policy, 216 Ostrom Ave., Syracuse, N.Y. 13210, is interested in studying and promoting services and life patterns which are as normal and nonstigmatizing as possible. Advocacy and training of professionals in the field of mental retardation and other disabilities are key components.
Disabled in Action, 175 Willoughby St., Brooklyn, N.Y. 11201, is a broadly based organization of disabled and nondisabled people working to guarantee the civil and inalienable rights of the nation's many millions of disabled individuals.

Publications to Write For

To get on the mailing list for inexpensive magazine subscriptions, write to:
Publishers Clearing House
Channel Drive
Port Washington, N.Y. 11050

To get on the mailing list for publishers' closeouts and new complete editions of books, prints and records, write:

Publishers Central Bureau

1 Champion Ave.

Avenel, N.J. 07131

If you want to regularly receive a list of publications put out by the U.S. government, write:

Superintendent of Documents

U.S. Government Printing Office

Washington, D.C. 20402

Barrier Free Design, Accessibility for the Handicapped is a free, 31-page booklet. Write:

The Institute for Research and Development in Occupational Education

The Graduate School of the University of New York

33 West 42nd St.

New York, N.Y. 10036

For a manual of exercise programs, self-help devices, and home-care procedures, get:

The Patient at Home by Marylou R. Barries and Carolyn A. Crutchfield

Charles B. Slack

6900 Grove Rd.

Thorofare, N.J. 08086

A good source for inexpensive pamphlets on most important subjects is:

Public Affairs Pamphlets

381 Park Ave. South

New York, N.Y. 10016

A good book for one-handed people is:

The One-Hander's Book: Helpful Hints for Activities of Daily Living by Veronica Washam

John Day

666 Fifth Ave.

New York, N.Y. 10019

An organization dedicated to developing reading skills:

Laubach Literacy, Inc.

Box 131

Syracuse, N.Y. 13210

For free information on food, write:

Food Is More Than Just Something to Eat

Nutrition USA

Pueblo, Colo. 81009

A famous relief organization you can trust for sure:
Care, Inc.
   660 First Ave.
   New York, N.Y. 10016
   Consumer information:
Consumer Information
   Pueblo, Colo. 81009
1001 Valuable Things You Can Get Free
   (Bantam paperback book that costs $1.25)
   Bantam Books
   666 Fifth Ave.
   New York, N.Y. 10019

For Legal Assistance

American Civil Liberties Union
   84 Fifth Ave.
   New York, N.Y. 10011
Center for Law and Social Policy
   1600 20th St., N.W.
   Washington, D.C. 20009
The Children's Defense Fund
   1763 R St., N.W.
   Washington, D.C. 20009
The National Center for Law and the Handicapped
   1235 North Eddy St.
   South Bend, Ind. 46617
National Legal Aid & Defender Association
   National Law Office
   1601 Connecticut Ave., N.W.
   Washington, D.C. 20009

Index